The Selected Poems of
William Carlos Williams

To Dick
From Jeanne
with love

By William Carlos Williams

The Autobiography
The Build-up
Collected Earlier Poems
Collected Later Poems
The Embodiment of Knowledge
The Farmers' Daughters
I Wanted to Write a Poem*
Imaginations
In the American Grain
In the Money
Interviews with William Carlos Williams
Kora in Hell: Improvisations†
Many Loves and Other Plays
Paterson, Books 1-5
Pictures from Brueghel and Other Poems
The Selected Essays
Selected Poems
A Voyage to Pagany
White Mule
The William Carlos Williams Reader

* *Beacon Press*
† *City Lights Books*

Selected Poems of

WILLIAM CARLOS WILLIAMS

With an Introduction by Randall Jarrell

A NEW DIRECTIONS PAPERBOOK

Copyright 1917, 1921 by The Four Seas Company. Copyright 1934 by The Objectivist Press. Copyright 1935 by The Alcestis Press. Copyright 1936 by Ronald Lane Latimer. Copyright 1938, 1941, 1944, 1946, 1948, 1949, 1950, 1951, 1952, 1953 and 1954 by William Carlos Williams. Copyright © 1955, 1956, 1957, 1959, 1960, 1961, and 1962 by William Carlos Williams. Copyright © 1969 by Florence Williams. Library of Congress Catalog Card Number: 69-11993.

ISBN: 0-8112-0236-4.

PUBLISHER'S NOTE: *The Selected Poems of William Carlos Williams* was first published in The New Classics Series in 1949. The selection of poems was made by Dr. Williams in consultation with the publisher and Randall Jarrell. First published paperbound in 1963. For this enlarged edition, published in 1968, poems were added from *The Desert Music* (1954), *Journey to Love* (1955) and *Pictures from Brueghel* (1962), chosen by Mrs. Williams and a committee of editorial advisers.

All rights reserved. Except for brief passages quoted in a newspaper, magazine, radio, or television review, no part of this book may be reproduced in any form or by any means, electronic or mechanical, including photocopying and recording, or by any information storage and retrieval system, without permission in writing from the Publisher.

Published in Canada by McClelland & Stewart, Ltd.

New Directions Books are published for James Laughlin by New Directions Publishing Corporation, 333 Sixth Avenue, New York 10014.

SEVENTH PRINTING

Contents

Introduction   ix

A Coronal   89
Adam   72
Aigeltinger   118
All the Fancy Things   43
A Marriage Ritual   93
A Negro Woman   156
An Elegy for D. H. Lawrence   64
An Exercise   165
Arrival   17
A Sort of a Song   108
FROM *Asphodel, That Greeny Flower*
    BOOK I   142
      CODA   151
At the Ball Game   31
A Unison   128

Between Walls   84
Burning the Christmas Greens   109

Choral: the Pink Church   122
Complaint   23

Danse Russe   5
Death   44
Dedication for a Plot of Ground   6

El Hombre   16

Fine Work with Pitch and Copper   70
Flowers by the Sea   63
Franklin Square   121

Great Mullen   22

Heel & Toe to the End   164

Impromptu: The Suckers   96
It Is a Living Coral   56

January Morning   1

Lear   126
Love Song   14

Nantucket   49

Ol' Bunk's Band   115
On Gay Wallpaper   54
Overture to a Dance of Locomotives   21

Pastoral   15
Paterson: Episode 17   85
Paterson: the Falls   112
Paul   168
Perpetuum Mobile: The City   78
FROM *Pictures from Brueghel*

    I SELF-PORTRAIT   159
    III THE HUNTERS IN THE SNOW   160
    VIII THE WEDDING DANCE IN THE OPEN AIR   161
    IX THE PARABLE OF THE BLIND   162
    X CHILDREN'S GAMES   163

Poem   54
Portrait of a Lady   35
Proletarian Portrait   63

Queen Anne's Lace   16

Rain   40
Raleigh Was Right   99

St. Francis Einstein of the Daffodils   75
Shadows   157
Smell!   11

Song 170
Spring and All 24
Spring Strains 9

The Attic Which Is Desire: 47
The Birds' Companion 32
The Botticellian Trees 48
The Bull 52
The Catholic Bells 61
The Clouds 100
The Cod Head 50
The Dance 113
The Dance 166
The Descent 132
The Descent of Winter 33
The Gift 171
*The High Bridge above the Tagus River
    at Toledo* 170
The Horse Show 127
The Hunter 18
The Injury 119
The Lady Speaks 155
*The Last Words of My English
    Grandmother* 94
The Lily 53
The Lion 130
The Locust Tree in Flower 68
The Lonely Street 20
The Poor 92
The Pot of Flowers 25
The Quality of Heaven 114
The Red Lily 45
The Red Wheelbarrow 30
The Rewaking 168
The Rose 26
The Sea-Elephant 36

The Semblables   105
The Snow Begins   167
The Sparrow   138
The Term   91
The Three Graces   131
The Trees   59
The Visit   116
FROM *The Wanderer: A Rococo Study*
    The Strike   7
The Widow's Lament in Springtime   17
The Wind Increases   69
The Woodthrush   173
The Yachts   71
The Yellow Chimney   104
The Young Housewife   77
These   90
This Is Just to Say   55
To a Poor Old Woman   67
To a Solitary Disciple   10
To Be Recited to Flossie on Her Birthday   174
To Daphne and Virginia   133
To Elsie   28
To Ford Madox Ford in Heaven   107
To Mark Anthony in Heaven   51
To Waken an Old Lady   19
Tract   12

Waiting   19

Young Sycamore   39

Introduction

An introduction to these poems can be useful to the reader in the way that an introduction to Peirce or William James can be: the reader is entering a realm that has some of the confusion and richness of the world, and any sort of summary is useful that keeps him reassured for a while—after that the place is its own justification. But most readers will automatically make any adjustments they need to make for writers so outspoken, good-hearted, and largely generous as Peirce and James and Williams. Just their voices are introduction enough: if an American doesn't understand these men, what will he understand?

Anyone would apply to Williams—besides *outspoken, good-hearted*, and *generous*—such words as *fresh, sympathetic, enthusiastic, spontaneous, open, impulsive, emotional, observant, curious, rash, courageous, undignified, unaffected, humanitarian, experimental, empirical, liberal, secular, democratic*. Both what he keeps and what he rejects are unusual: how many of these words would fit the other good poets of the time? He was born younger than they, with more of the frontier about him, of the this-worldly optimism of the 18th century; one can imagine his reading *Rameau's Nephew* with delighted enthusiasm, but wading along in Karl Barth with a dour blank frown. (I don't mean to dissociate myself from these responses.) And he is as Pelagian as an obstetrician should be: as he points to the poor red thing mewling behind plateglass, he says with professional, observant disbelief: "You mean you think *that*'s full of Original Sin?" He has the honesty that consists in writing down the way things seem to you yourself, not the way that they really must be, that they *are*, that everybody but a misguided idealist or shallow optimist or bourgeois sentimentalist *knows* they are. One has about him the amused, admiring, and affectionate certainty that one has about Whitman: *Why, he'd say anything!*—creditable or discreditable, sayable or unsayable, so long as he believes it. There is something particularly willing and generous about the man in and behind the poems: one is attracted to him so automatically that one is "reminded of a story" of how S____ was defined as the only man in the universe who didn't like William James.

A *Selected Poems* like this does far less than justice to Williams. Any fair selection would have to include his wonderful book-length poem *Paterson;* and Williams is one of those poets, like Hardy, whose bad or mediocre poems do repay reading and do add to your respect for the poet. Williams' bad poems are usually rather winning machine-parts minus their machine, irrepressible exclamations about the weather of the world, interesting but more or less autonomous and irrelevant entries in a Lifetime Diary. But this is attractive; the usual bad poem in somebody's *Collected Works* is a learned, mannered, valued habit —a habit a little more careful than, and a little emptier than, brushing one's teeth.

The first thing one notices about Williams's poetry is how radically sensational and perceptual it is: "Say it! No ideas but in things." Williams shares with Marianne Moore and Wallace Stevens a feeling that almost nothing is more important, more of a true delight, than the way things look. Reading their poems is one long shudder of recognition; their reproduction of things, in its empirical gaiety, its clear abstract refinement of presentation, has something peculiarly and paradoxically American about it—English readers usually talk about their work as if it had been produced by three triangles fresh from Flatland. All three of these poets might have used, as an epigraph for their poetry, Goethe's beautiful saying that it is nicer to think than to do, to feel than to think, but nicest of all merely to look. Williams's poems, so far as their spirit is concerned, remind one of Marianne Moore's "It is not the plunder,/ but 'accessibility to experience' "; so far as their letter is concerned, they carry scrawled all over them Stevens's "The greatest poverty is not to live/ In a physical world"—and Stevens continues, quite as if he were Williams looking with wondering love at all the unlikely beauties of the poor:

One might have thought of sight, but who could think
Of what it sees, for all the ill it sees.

All three poets did their first good work in an odd climate of poetic opinion. Its expectations of behavior were imagist (the poet is supposed to see everything, to feel a great deal, and to think and to do and to make hardly anything), its metrical demands were minimal, and its ideals of organization were mosaic. The subject of poetry had changed from the actions of men to the reactions of poets—*reactions* being defined in a way that left the poet almost without motor system or cerebral cortex. This easily led to a strange kind of abstraction: for what is more abstract than a fortuitous collocation of sensations? Stevens, with his passion for philosophy, order, and blank verse, was naturally least affected by the atmosphere of the time, in which he was at most a tourist; and Marianne Moore synthesized her own novel organization out of syllabic verse, extravagantly elaborated, half-visual patterns, and an extension of moral judgment, feeling, and generalization to the whole world of imagist perception. Williams found his own sort of imagism considerably harder to modify. He had a boyish delight and trust in Things: there is always on his lips the familiar, pragmatic, American *These are the facts*—for he is the most pragmatic of writers, and so American that the adjective itself seems inadequate . . . one exclaims in despair and delight: He is the America of poets. Few of his poems had that pure crystalline inconsequence that the imagist poem ideally has—the world and Williams himself kept breaking into them; and this was certainly their salvation.

Williams's poetry is more remarkable for its empathy, sympathy, its muscular and emotional identification with its subjects, than any other contemporary poetry except Rilke's. When you have read *Paterson* you know for the rest of your life what it is like to be a waterfall; and what other poet has turned so many of his readers into trees? Occasionally one realizes that this latest tree of Williams's is considerably more active than anybody else's grizzly bear; but usually the identification is so natural, the feel and rhythm of the poem so hypnotic, that the problem of belief never arises. Williams's knowledge of plants and animals, our brothers and sisters in the world, is surprising for its range and intensity; and he sets them down in the midst of the real weather of the world, so that the reader is full of an innocent lyric pleasure just in being out in the open, in feeling the wind tickling his skin. The poems are full of "Nature": Williams has reproduced with exact and loving fidelity both the illumination of the letter and the movement of the spirit. In these poems emotions, ideals, whole atttiudes are implicit in a tone of voice, in the feel of his own overheard speech; or are expressed in terms of plants, animals, the landscape, the weather. You see from his instructions "To a Solitary Disciple" that it is what the landscape *does*—its analogical, anthropomorphized life—that matters to Williams; and it is only as the colors and surfaces reveal this that they are important.

At first people were introduced into the poems mainly as overheard or overlooked landscape; they spread. Williams has the knowledge of people one expects, and often does not get, from doctors; a knowledge one does not expect, and almost never gets, from contemporary poets. (For instance, what is probably the best poem of our time, *Four Quartets*, has only one real character, the poet, and a recurrent state of that character which we are assured is God; even the ghostly mentor encountered after the air-raid is half Eliot himself, a sort of Dostoievsky double.) One believes in and remembers the people in Williams's poems, though they usually remain behavioristic, sharply observed, sympathetic and empathetic sketches, and one cannot expect from these sketches the knowledge of a character that one gets from some of Frost's early dramatic monologues and narratives, from a number of Hardy's poems, or from Williams's detailed and conclusive treatment of the most interesting character in his poems, himself. Some of the narrative and dramatic elements of his poetry seem to have drained off into his fiction. Williams's attitude toward his people is particularly admirable: he has neither that condescending, impatient, Pharisaical dismissal of the illiterate mass of mankind, nor that manufactured, mooing awe for an equally manufactured Little or Common Man, that disfigures so much contemporary writing. Williams loves, blames, and yells despairingly at the Little Men just as naturally and legitimately as Saint-Loup got angry at the servants: because he *feels*, not just says, that the differences between men are less important than their similarities—that he and you and I, together, are the Little Men.

Williams has a real and unusual dislike of, distrust in, Authority; and the Father-surrogate of the average work of art has been banished from his Eden. His ability to rest (or at least to thrash happily about) in contradiction, doubts, and general guesswork, without ever climbing aboard any of the monumental certainties that go perpetually by, perpetually on time—this ability may seem the opposite of Whitman's gift for boarding every certainty and riding off into every infinite, but the spirit behind them is the same. Williams's range (it is roughly Paterson, that microcosm which he has half-discovered, half-invented) is narrower than Whitman's, and yet there too one is reminded of Whitman: Williams has much of the freeness of an earlier America, though it is a freedom haunted about by desperation and sorrow. The little motto one could invent for him—*In the suburbs, there one feels free*—is particularly ambiguous when one considers that those suburbs of his are overshadowed by, are a part of, the terrible industrial landscape of northeastern New Jersey. But the ambiguity is one that Williams himself not only understands but insists upon: if his poems are full of what is clear, delicate, and beautiful, they are also full of what is coarse, ugly, and horrible. There is no optimistic blindness in Williams, though there is a fresh gaiety, a stubborn or invincible joyousness. But when one thinks of the poems, of Williams himself, in the midst of these factories, dumps, subdivisions, express highways, patients, children, weeds, and flowers of theirs—with the city of New York rising before them on the horizon, a pillar of smoke by day, a pillar of fire by night; when one thinks of this, one sees in an ironic light, the flat matter-of-fact light of the American landscapes, James' remark that America "has no ruins." America is full of ruins, the ruins of hopes.

There are continually apparent in Williams that delicacy and subtlety which are sometimes so extraordinarily present, and sometimes so extraordinarily absent, in Whitman; and the hair-raising originality of some of Whitman's language is another bond between the two—one thinks of Williams as one reads

The orchestra whirls me wider than Uranus flies,
It wrenches such ardors from me I did not know I possessed them,
It sails me, I dab with bare feet, they are lick'd by the indolent waves,
I am cut by bitter and angry hail, I lose my breath,
Steep'd amid honey'd morphine, my windpipe throttled in fakes of death,
At length let up again to feel the puzzle of puzzles ...

In spite of their faults—some of them obvious to, and some of them seductive to, the most foolish reader—poets like Whitman and Williams have about them something more valuable than any faultlessness: a wonderful largeness, a quantitative and qualitative generosity.

Williams's imagist-objectivist background and bias have helped his poems by their emphasis on truthfulness, exactness, concrete "presentation"; but they have harmed the poems by their underemphasis on organization, logic, narrative, generalization—and the poems are so short, often, that there isn't time for much. Some of the poems seem to say, "Truth is enough"—*truth* meaning *data brought back alive*. But truth isn't enough. Our crudest demand for excitement, for "the actions of men," for the "real story" of something "important," something strange—this demand is legitimate because it is the nature of the animal, man, to make it; and the demand can hardly be neglected so much as a great deal of the poetry of our time—of the good poetry of our time—has neglected it. The materials of Williams's unsuccessful poems have as much reality as the brick one stumbles over on the sidewalk; but how little has been done to them!—the poem is pieces or, worse still, a piece. But sometimes just enough, exactly as little as is necessary, has been done; and in these poems the Nature of the edge of the American city —the weeds, clouds, and children of vacant lots—and its reflection in the minds of its inhabitants, exist for good.

One accepts as a perfect criticism of his own insufficiently organized (i. e., insufficiently living) poems Williams's own lines: "And we thought to escape rime/ by imitation of the senseless/ unarrangement of wild things—the stupidest rime of all"; and one realizes at the same time, with a sense of assurance, that few people know better than Williams how sensible the arrangement of wild things often is. Williams's good poems are in perfect agreement with his own intelligent and characteristic explanation of what a poem is:

"A poem is a small (or large) machine made of words. When I say there's nothing sentimental about a poem I mean that there can be no part, as in any other machine, that is redundant . . . Its movement is intrinsic, undulant, a physical more than a literary character. Therefore each speech having its own character, the poetry it engenders will be peculiar to that speech also in its own intrinsic form. The effect is beauty, what in a single object resolves our complex feelings of propriety . . . When a man makes a poem, makes it, mind you, he takes words as he finds them interrelated about him and composes them—without distortion which would mar their exact significances—into an intense expression of his perceptions and ardors that they may constitute a revelation in the speech that he uses. It isn't what he *says* that counts as a work of art, it's what he makes, with such intensity of perception that it lives with an intrinsic movement of its own to verify its authenticity."

One is rather embarrassed at the necessity of calling Williams original; it is like saying that a Cheshire Cat smiles. Originality is one of his major virtues and minor vices. One thinks about some of his best poems, *I've never read or imagined anything like this;* and one thinks about some of his worst, *I wish to God this were a little more like ordinary poetry.* He is even less logical than the average good poet—he is an "intellectual" in neither the good nor the bad sense of the word—but loves abstractions for their own sakes, and makes accomplished, characteristic, inveterate use of them, exactly as if they were sensations or emotions; there is no "dissociation of sensibility" in Williams. Both generalizations and particulars are handled with freshness and humor and imagination, with a delicacy and fantasy that are especially charming in so vigorous, realistic, and colloquial a writer.

The mosaic organization characteristic of imagism or "objectivism" develops naturally into the musical, thematic organization of longer poems like *Paterson;* many of its structural devices are interestingly close to those of *Four Quartets* and "Coriolan," though Eliot at the same time utilizes a good many of the traditional devices that Williams dislikes. A large-scale organization which is neither logical, dramatic, nor narrative is something that contemporary poetry has particularly desired; such an organization seems possible but improbable, does not exist at present, and is most nearly approached in *Four Quartets* and *Paterson.*

Williams's poems are full of imperatives, exclamations, trochees—the rhythms and dynamics of their speech are being insisted upon as they could not be in any prose: it is this insistence upon dynamics that is fundamental in Williams's reading of his own poems. You've never heard a Williams poem until you've heard him read it; the listener realizes with astonished joy that he is hearing a method of reading poetry that is both excellent and completely unlike anything he has ever heard before. About Williams's meters one remark might be enough, here: that no one has written more accomplished and successful free verse. It seems to me that ordinary accentual-syllabic verse, in general, has tremendous advantages over "free," accentual, or syllabic verse. But that these other kinds of verse, in some particular situations or with some particular materials, can work out better for some poets, is so plain that any assertion to the contrary seems obstinate dogmatism. We want to explain *why* Williams's free verse or Marianne Moore's syllabic verse is successful, not to make fools of ourselves by arguing that it isn't. The verse-form of one of their poems, as anyone can see, is essential to its success; and it is impossible to produce the same effect by treating their material in accentual-syllabic verse. Anyone can invent the genius who might have done the whole thing even better in ordinary English verse, but he is the most fruitless of inventions.*

Contemporary criticism has not done very well by Williams; most of the good critics of poetry have not written about him, and one or two of the best, when they did write, just twitched as if flies were crawling over them. Yvor Winters has been Williams's most valuable advocate, and has written extremely well about one side of Williams's poetry;

---

* Randall Jarrell's introduction was written in 1949, before Williams had much publicized his metrical theories of the "variable foot" and the triadic line. About 1961, when Paul Engle and Joseph Langland asked Williams to designate his favorite poem for their *Poet's Choice* anthology, he chose *The Descent*, saying: "I write in the American Idiom and for many years I have been using what I call the variable foot. 'The Descent' is the first poem in that medium that wholly satisfied me."—*Publisher*

but his praise has never had enough effect on the average reader, who felt that Williams came as part of the big economy-sized package that included Elizabeth Daryush, Jones Very, and Winters' six best students. The most important thing that criticism can do for a contemporary poet is to establish that atmosphere of interested respect which gets his poems a reasonably careful reading; it is only in the last couple of years that any such atmosphere has been established for Williams.

Williams's most impressive single piece is certainly *Paterson:* a reader has to be determinedly insensitive to modern poetry not to see that it has an extraordinary range and reality, a clear rightness that sometimes approaches perfection. I imagine that almost any list of Williams's best poems would include the extremely moving, completely realized "The Widow's Lament in Springtime"; that terrible poem which begins, *The pure products of America/ go crazy* (Section XVIII of "Spring and All"); "The Yachts," a poem that is a paradigm of all the unjust beauty, the necessary and unnecessary injustice of the world; "These," a poem that is pure deprivation; "Burning the Christmas Greens"; the long poem (called "Paterson: Episode from Book III") that uses for a refrain the phrase *Beautiful Thing;* the unimaginably delicate "To Waken an Old Lady"; the poem that begins *By the road to the contagious hospital* (Section I of "Spring and All"); the wonderful "A Unison," in which Nature once again becomes for us both ritual and myth; and, perhaps, "The Sea-Elephant," "The Semblables," and "The Injury." And how many other poems there are that one never comes on without pleasure!

That Williams's poems are honest, exact, and original, that some of them are really *good* poems, seems to me obvious. But in concluding I had rather mention something even more obvious: their generosity and sympathy, their moral and human attractiveness.

—*Randall Jarrell*
1949

January Morning

SUITE:

I

I have discovered that most of
the beauties of travel are due to
the strange hours we keep to see them:

the domes of the Church of
the Paulist Fathers in Weehawken
against a smoky dawn—the heart stirred—
are beautiful as Saint Peters
approached after years of anticipation.

II

Though the operation was postponed
I saw the tall probationers
in their tan uniforms
                hurrying to breakfast!

III

—and from basement entries
neatly coiffed, middle aged gentlemen
with orderly moustaches and
well-brushed coats

IV

—and the sun, dipping into the avenues
streaking the tops of

the irregular red houselets,
                                    and
the gay shadows dropping and dropping.

V

—and a young horse with a green bed-quilt
on his withers shaking his head:
bared teeth and nozzle high in the air!

VI

—and a semicircle of dirt-colored men
about a fire bursting from an old
ash can,

VII

            —and the worn,
blue car rails (like the sky!)
gleaming among the cobbles!

VIII

—and the rickety ferry-boat "Arden"!
What an object to be called "Arden"
among the great piers,—on the
ever new river!
            "Put me a Touchstone
at the wheel, white gulls, and we'll
follow the ghost of the *Half Moon*
to the North West Passage—and through!
(at Albany!) for all that!"

IX

Exquisite brown waves—long
circlets of silver moving over you!
enough with crumbling ice crusts among you!
The sky has come down to you,
lighter than tiny bubbles, face to
face with you!
                His spirit is
a white gull with delicate pink feet
and a snowy breast for you to
hold to your lips delicately!

X

The young doctor is dancing with happiness
in the sparkling wind, alone
at the prow of the ferry! He notices
the curdy barnacles and broken ice crusts
left at the slip's base by the low tide
and thinks of summer and green
shell-crusted ledges among
                    the emerald eel-grass!

XI

Who knows the Palisades as I do
knows the river breaks east from them
above the city—but they continue south
—under the sky—to bear a crest of
little peering houses that brighten
with dawn behind the moody
water-loving giants of Manhattan.

XII

Long yellow rushes bending
above the white snow patches;
purple and gold ribbon
of the distant wood:
         what an angle
you make with each other as
you lie there in contemplation.

XIII

Work hard all your young days
and they'll find you too, some morning
staring up under
your chiffonier at its warped
bass-wood bottom and your soul—
out!
—among the little sparrows
behind the shutter.

XIV

—and the flapping flags are at
half mast for the dead admiral.

XV

All this—
        was for you, old woman.
I wanted to write a poem
that you would understand.
For what good is it to me

if you can't understand it?
     But you got to try hard—
But—
 Well, you know how
the young girls run giggling
on Park Avenue after dark
when they ought to be home in bed?
Well,
that's the way it is with me somehow.

Danse Russe

    If when my wife is sleeping
    and the baby and Kathleen
    are sleeping
    and the sun is a flame-white disc
    in silken mists
    above shining trees,—
    if I in my north room
    dance naked, grotesquely
    before my mirror
    waving my shirt round my head
    and singing softly to myself:
    "I am lonely, lonely.
    I was born to be lonely,
    I am best so!"
    If I admire my arms, my face,
    my shoulders, flanks, buttocks
    against the yellow drawn shades,—

    Who shall say I am not
    the happy genius of my household?

Dedication for a Plot of Ground

This plot of ground
facing the waters of this inlet
is dedicated to the living presence of
Emily Dickinson Wellcome
who was born in England, married,
lost her husband and with
her five year old son
sailed for New York in a two-master,
was driven to the Azores;
ran adrift on Fire Island shoal,
met her second husband
in a Brooklyn boarding house,
went with him to Puerto Rico
bore three more children, lost
her second husband, lived hard
for eight years in St. Thomas,
Puerto Rico, San Domingo, followed
the oldest son to New York,
lost her daughter, lost her "baby",
seized the two boys of
the oldest son by the second marriage
mothered them—they being
motherless—fought for them
against the other grandmother
and the aunts, brought them here
summer after summer, defended
herself here against thieves,
storms, sun, fire,
against flies, against girls
that came smelling about, against
drought, against weeds, storm-tides,
neighbors, weasels that stole her chickens,
against the weakness of her own hands,

against the growing strength of
the boys, against wind, against
the stones, against trespassers,
against rents, against her own mind.

She grubbed this earth with her own hands,
domineered over this grass plot,
blackguarded her oldest son
into buying it, lived here fifteen years,
attained a final loneliness and—

If you can bring nothing to this place
but your carcass, keep out.

From **The Wanderer: A Rococo Study**

THE STRIKE

At the first peep of dawn she roused me!
I rose trembling at the change which the night saw!
For there, wretchedly brooding in a corner
From which her old eyes glittered fiercely—
"Go!" she said, and I hurried shivering
Out into the deserted streets of Paterson.
That night she came again, hovering
In rags within the filmy ceiling—
"Great Queen, bless me with thy tatters!"
"You are blest, go on!"
                            "Hot for savagery,
Sucking the air! I went into the city,
Out again, baffled onto the mountain!
Back into the city!
                    Nowhere
The subtle! Everywhere the electric!"

"A short bread-line before a hitherto empty tea shop:
No questions—all stood patiently,
Dominated by one idea: something
That carried them as they are always wanting to be carried,
'But what is it,' I asked those nearest me,
'This thing heretofore unobtainable
'That they seem so clever to have put on now!'

"Why since I have failed them can it be anything but their
    own brood?
Can it be anything but brutality?
On that at least they're united! That at least
Is their bean soup, their calm bread and a few luxuries!

"But in me, more sensitive, marvelous old queen
It sank deep into the blood, that I rose upon
The tense air enjoying the dusty fight!
Heavy drink where the low, sloping foreheads
The flat skulls with the unkempt black or blond hair,
The ugly legs of the young girls, pistons
Too powerful for delicacy!
The women's wrists, the men's arms red
Used to heat and cold, to toss quartered beeves
And barrels, and milk-cans, and crates of fruit!

"Faces all knotted up like burls on oaks,
Grasping, fox-snouted, thick-lipped,
Sagging breasts and protruding stomachs,
Rasping voices, filthy habits with the hands.
Nowhere you! Everywhere the electric!

"Ugly, venomous, gigantic!
Tossing me as a great father his helpless
Infant till it shriek with ecstasy
And its eyes roll and its tongue hangs out!—

"I am at peace again, old queen, I listen clearer now."

Spring Strains

In a tissue-thin monotone of blue-grey buds
crowded erect with desire against the sky—
      tense blue-grey twigs
slenderly anchoring them down, drawing
them in—

      two blue-grey birds chasing
a third struggle in circles, angles,
swift convergings to a point that bursts
instantly!

    Vibrant bowing limbs
pull downward, sucking in the sky
that bulges from behind, plastering itself
against them in packed rifts, rock blue
and dirty orange!

                        But—
(Hold hard, rigid jointed trees!)
the blinding and red-edged sun-blur—
creeping energy, concentrated
counterforce—welds sky, buds, trees,
rivets them in one puckering hold!
Sticks through! Pulls the whole
counter-pulling mass upward, to the right
locks even the opaque, not yet defined
ground in a terrific drag that is
loosening the very tap-roots!

On a tissue-thin monotone of blue-grey buds
two blue-grey birds, chasing a third,
at full cry! Now they are
flung outward and up—disappearing suddenly!

To a Solitary Disciple

Rather notice, mon cher,
that the moon is
tilted above
the point of the steeple
than that its color
is shell-pink.

Rather observe
that it is early morning
than that the sky
is smooth
as a turquoise.

Rather grasp
how the dark
converging lines
of the steeple
meet at the pinnacle—
perceive how
its little ornament
tries to stop them—

See how it fails!
See how the converging lines
of the hexagonal spire
escape upward—
receding, dividing!
—sepals
that guard and contain
the flower!

Observe
how motionless

        the eaten moon
        lies in the protecting lines.
        It is true:
        in the light colors
        of morning

        brown-stone and slate
        shine orange and dark blue.

        But observe
        the oppressive weight
        of the squat edifice!
        Observe
        the jasmine lightness
        of the moon.

Smell!

Oh strong-ridged and deeply hollowed
nose of mine! what will you not be smelling?
What tactless asses we are, you and I boney nose
always indiscriminate, always unashamed,
and now it is the souring flowers of the bedraggled
poplars: a festering pulp on the wet earth
beneath them. With what deep thirst
we quicken our desires
to that rank odor of a passing springtime!
Can you not be decent? Can you not reserve your ardors
for something less unlovely? What girl will care
for us, do you think, if we continue in these ways?
Must you taste everything? Must you know everything?
Must you have a part in everything?

Tract

I will teach you my townspeople
how to perform a funeral
for you have it over a troop
of artists—
unless one should scour the world—
you have the ground sense necessary.

See! the hearse leads.
I begin with a design for a hearse.
For Christ's sake not black—
nor white either—and not polished!
Let it be weathered—like a farm wagon—
with gilt wheels (this could be
applied fresh at small expense)
or no wheels at all:
a rough dray to drag over the ground.

Knock the glass out!
My God—glass, my townspeople!
For what purpose? Is it for the dead
to look out or for us to see
how well he is housed or to see
the flowers or the lack of them—
or what?
To keep the rain and snow from him?
He will have a heavier rain soon:
pebbles and dirt and what not.
Let there be no glass—
and no upholstery, phew!
and no little brass rollers
and small easy wheels on the bottom—
my townspeople what are you thinking of?

A rough plain hearse then
with gilt wheels and no top at all.
On this the coffin lies
by its own weight.

                    No wreaths please—
especially no hot house flowers.
Some common memento is better,
something he prized and is known by:
his old clothes—a few books perhaps—
God knows what! You realize
how we are about these things
my townspeople—
something will be found—anything
even flowers if he had come to that.
So much for the hearse.

For heaven's sake though see to the driver!
Take off the silk hat! In fact
that's no place at all for him—
up there unceremoniously
dragging our friend out to his own dignity!
Bring him down—bring him down!
Low and inconspicuous! I'd not have him ride
on the wagon at all—damn him—
the undertaker's understrapper!
Let him hold the reins
and walk at the side
and inconspicuously too!

Then briefly as to yourselves:
Walk behind—as they do in France,
seventh class, or if you ride
Hell take curtains! Go with some show
of inconvenience; sit openly—
to the weather as to grief.

Or do you think you can shut grief in?
What—from us? We who have perhaps
nothing to lose? Share with us
share with us—it will be money
in your pockets.
                        Go now
I think you are ready.

Love Song

        I lie here thinking of you:—

        the stain of love
        is upon the world!
        Yellow, yellow, yellow
        it eats into the leaves,
        smears with saffron
        the horned branches that lean
        heavily
        against a smooth purple sky!
        There is no light
        only a honey-thick stain
        that drips from leaf to leaf
        and limb to limb
        spoiling the colors
        of the whole world—

        you far off there under
        the wine-red selvage of the west!

Pastoral

> The little sparrows
> hop ingenuously
> about the pavement
> quarreling
> with sharp voices
> over those things
> that interest them.
> But we who are wiser
> shut ourselves in
> on either hand
> and no one knows
> whether we think good
> or evil.
>
>   Meanwhile,
> the old man who goes about
> gathering dog-lime
> walks in the gutter
> without looking up
> and his tread
> is more majestic than
> that of the Episcopal minister
> approaching the pulpit
> of a Sunday.
>   These things
> astonish me beyond words.

El Hombre

It's a strange courage
you give me ancient star:

Shine alone in the sunrise
toward which you lend no part!

Queen Anne's Lace

Her body is not so white as
anemone petals nor so smooth—nor
so remote a thing. It is a field
of the wild carrot taking
the field by force; the grass
does not raise above it.
Here is no question of whiteness,
white as can be, with a purple mole
at the center of each flower.
Each flower is a hand's span
of her whiteness. Wherever
his hand has lain there is
a tiny purple blemish. Each part
is a blossom under his touch
to which the fibres of her being
stem one by one, each to its end,
until the whole field is a
white desire, empty, a single stem,
a cluster, flower by flower,
a pious wish to whiteness gone over—
or nothing.

Arrival

And yet one arrives somehow,
finds himself loosening the hooks of
her dress
in a strange bedroom—
feels the autumn
dropping its silk and linen leaves
about her ankles.
The tawdry veined body emerges
twisted upon itself
like a winter wind . . . !

The Widow's Lament in Springtime

Sorrow is my own yard
where the new grass
flames as it has flamed
often before but not
with the cold fire
that closes round me this year.
Thirtyfive years
I lived with my husband.
The plumtree is white today
with masses of flowers.
Masses of flowers
load the cherry branches
and color some bushes
yellow and some red
but the grief in my heart
is stronger than they
for though they were my joy

formerly, today I notice them
and turned away forgetting.
Today my son told me
that in the meadows,
at the edge of the heavy woods
in the distance, he saw
trees of white flowers.
I feel that I would like
to go there
and fall into those flowers
and sink into the marsh near them.

The Hunter

In the flashes and black shadows
of July
the days, locked in each other's arms,
seem still
so that squirrels and colored birds
go about at ease over
the branches and through the air.

Where will a shoulder split or
a forehead open and victory be?

Nowhere.
Both sides grow older.

And you may be sure
not one leaf will lift itself
from the ground
and become fast to a twig again.

To Waken An Old Lady

Old age is
a flight of small
cheeping birds
skimming
bare trees
above a snow glaze.
Gaining and failing
they are buffeted
by a dark wind—
But what?
On harsh weedstalks
the flock has rested,
the snow
is covered with broken
seedhusks
and the wind tempered
by a shrill
piping of plenty.

Waiting

When I am alone I am happy.
The air is cool. The sky is
flecked and splashed and wound
with color. The crimson phalloi
of the sassafras leaves
hang crowded before me
in shoals on the heavy branches.
When I reach my doorstep

I am greeted by
the happy shrieks of my children
and my heart sinks.
I am crushed.

Are not my children as dear to me
as falling leaves or
must one become stupid
to grow older?
It seems much as if Sorrow
had tripped up my heels.
Let us see, let us see!
What did I plan to say to her
when it should happen to me
as it has happened now?

The Lonely Street

School is over. It is too hot
to walk at ease. At ease
in light frocks they walk the streets
to while the time away.
They have grown tall. They hold
pink flames in their right hands.
In white from head to foot,
with sidelong, idle look—
in yellow, floating stuff,
black sash and stockings—
touching their avid mouths
with pink sugar on a stick—
like a carnation each holds in her hand—
they mount the lonely street.

Overture to a Dance of Locomotives

I

Men with picked voices chant the names
of cities in a huge gallery: promises
that pull through descending stairways
to a deep rumbling.

                The rubbing feet
of those coming to be carried quicken a
grey pavement into soft light that rocks
to and fro, under the domed ceiling,
across and across from pale
earthcolored walls of bare limestone.

Covertly the hands of a great clock
go round and round! Were they to
move quickly and at once the whole
secret would be out and the shuffling
of all ants be done forever.

A leaning pyramid of sunlight, narrowing
out at a high window, moves by the clock;
discordant hands straining out from
a center: inevitable postures infinitely
repeated—

two—twofour—twoeight!

Porters in red hats run on narrow platforms.

This way ma'am!
                —important not to take
the wrong train!

                    Lights from the concrete
ceiling hang crooked but—
                        Poised horizontal
on glittering parallels the dingy cylinders
packed with a warm glow—inviting entry—
pull against the hour. But brakes can
hold a fixed posture till—
                        The whistle!

Not twoeight. Not twofour. Two!

Gliding windows. Colored cooks sweating
in a small kitchen. Taillights—
In time: twofour!
In time: twoeight!

—rivers are tunneled: trestles
cross oozy swampland: wheels repeating
the same gesture remain relatively
stationary: rails forever parallel
return on themselves infinitely.
                        The dance is sure.

Great Mullen

One leaves his leaves at home
being a mullen and sends up a lighthouse
to peer from: I will have my way,
yellow—A mast with a lantern, ten
fifty, a hundred, smaller and smaller
as they grow more—Liar, liar, liar!
You come from her! I can smell djer-kiss

on your clothes. Ha! you come to me,
you—I am a point of dew on a grass-stem.
Why are you sending heat down on me
from your lantern?—You are cowdung, a
dead stick with the bark off. She is
squirting on us both. She has had her
hand on you!—well?—She has defiled
ME.—Your leaves are dull, thick
and hairy.—Every hair on my body will
hold you off from me. You are a
dungcake, birdlime on a fencerail.—
I love you, straight, yellow
finger of God pointing to—her!
Liar, broken weed, dungcake, you have—
I am a cricket waving his antennae
and you are high, grey and straight. Ha!

Complaint

They call me and I go.
It is a frozen road
past midnight, a dust
of snow caught
in the rigid wheeltracks.
The door opens.
I smile, enter and
shake off the cold.
Here is a great woman
on her side in the bed.
She is sick,
perhaps vomiting,
perhaps laboring

>   to give birth to
>   a tenth child. Joy! Joy!
>   Night is a room
>   darkened for lovers,
>   through the jalousies the sun
>   has sent one gold needle!
>   I pick the hair from her eyes
>   and watch her misery
>   with compassion.

From *Spring and All*

I

Spring and All

>   By the road to the contagious hospital
>   under the surge of the blue
>   mottled clouds driven from the
>   northeast—a cold wind. Beyond, the
>   waste of broad, muddy fields
>   brown with dried weeds, standing and fallen
>
>   patches of standing water
>   the scattering of tall trees
>
>   All along the road the reddish
>   purplish, forked, upstanding, twiggy
>   stuff of bushes and small trees
>   with dead, brown leaves under them
>   leafless vines—

Lifeless in appearance, sluggish
dazed spring approaches—

They enter the new world naked,
cold, uncertain of all
save that they enter. All about them
the cold, familiar wind—

Now the grass, tomorrow
the stiff curl of wildcarrot leaf
One by one objects are defined—
It quickens: clarity, outline of leaf

But now the stark dignity of
entrance—Still, the profound change
has come upon them: rooted, they
grip down and begin to awaken

II

The Pot of Flowers

Pink confused with white
flowers and flowers reversed
take and spill the shaded flame
darting it back
into the lamp's horn

petals aslant darkened with mauve

red where in whorls
petal lays its glow upon petal
round flamegreen throats

petals radiant with transpiercing light
contending
        above
the leaves
reaching up their modest green
from the pot's rim

and there, wholly dark, the pot
gay with rough moss.

VII

The Rose

The rose is obsolete
but each petal ends in
an edge, the double facet
cementing the grooved
columns of air—The edge
cuts without cutting
meets—nothing—renews
itself in metal or porcelain—

whither? It ends—

But if it ends
the start is begun
so that to engage roses
becomes a geometry—

Sharper, neater, more cutting
figured in majolica—
the broken plate
glazed with a rose

Somewhere the sense
makes copper roses
steel roses—

The rose carried weight of love
but love is at an end—of roses
It is at the edge of the
petal that love waits

Crisp, worked to defeat
laboredness—fragile
plucked, moist, half-raised
cold, precise, touching

What

The place between the petal's
edge and the

From the petal's edge a line starts
that being of steel
infinitely fine, infinitely
rigid penetrates
the Milky Way
without contact—lifting
from it—neither hanging
nor pushing—

The fragility of the flower
unbruised
penetrates space.

XVIII

To Elsie

The pure products of America
go crazy—
mountain folk from Kentucky

or the ribbed north end of
Jersey
with its isolate lakes and

valleys, its deaf-mutes, thieves
old names
and promiscuity between

devil-may-care men who have taken
to railroading
out of sheer lust of adventure—

and young slatterns, bathed
in filth
from Monday to Saturday

to be tricked out that night
with gauds
from imaginations which have no

peasant traditions to give them
character
but flutter and flaunt

sheer rags—succumbing without
emotion
save numbed terror

under some hedge of choke-cherry
or viburnum—
which they cannot express—

Unless it be that marriage
perhaps
with a dash of Indian blood

will throw up a girl so desolate
so hemmed round
with disease or murder

that she'll be rescued by an
agent—
reared by the state and

sent out at fifteen to work in
some hard-pressed
house in the suburbs—

some doctor's family, some Elsie—
voluptuous water
expressing with broken

brain the truth about us—
her great
ungainly hips and flopping breasts

addressed to cheap
jewelry
and rich young men with fine eyes

as if the earth under our feet
were
an excrement of some sky

and we degraded prisoners
destined
to hunger until we eat filth

while the imagination strains
after deer
going by fields of goldenrod in

the stifling heat of September
Somehow
it seems to destroy us

It is only in isolate flecks that
something
is given off

No one
to witness
and adjust, no one to drive the car

XXI *The Red Wheelbarrow*

      so much depends
      upon

      a red wheel
      barrow

      glazed with rain
      water

      beside the white
      chickens.

XXVI *At the Ball Game*

The crowd at the ball game
is moved uniformly

by a spirit of uselessness
which delights them—

all the exciting detail
of the chase

and the escape, the error
the flash of genius—

all to no end save beauty
the eternal—

So in detail they, the crowd,
are beautiful

for this
to be warned against

saluted and defied—
It is alive, venomous

it smiles grimly
its words cut—

The flashy female with her
mother, gets it—

The Jew gets it straight—it
is deadly, terrifying—

It is the Inquisition, the
Revolution

It is beauty itself
that lives

day by day in them
idly—

This is
the power of their faces

It is summer, it is the solstice
the crowd is

cheering, the crowd is laughing
in detail

permanently, seriously
without thought

The Bird's Companion

As love
    that is
each day upon the twig
    which may die

    So springs your love
fresh up
    lusty for the sun
the bird's companion—

The Descent of Winter

9/30

There are no perfect waves—
Your writings are a sea
full of misspellings and
faulty sentences. Level. Troubled

A center distant from the land
touched by the wings
of nearly silent birds
that never seem to rest—

This is the sadness of the sea—
waves like words, all broken—
a sameness of lifting and falling mood.

I lean watching the detail
of brittle crest, the delicate
imperfect foam, yellow weed
one piece like another—

There is no hope—if not a coral
island slowly forming
to wait for birds to drop
the seeds will make it habitable

10/22

that brilliant field
of rainwet orange
blanketed

by the red grass
and oilgreen bayberry

the last yarrow
on the gutter
white by the sandy
rainwater

and a white birch
with yellow leaves
and few
and loosely hung

and a young dog
jumped out
of the old barrel

10/28

in this strong light
the leafless beechtree
shines like a cloud

it seems to glow
of itself
with a soft stript light
of love
over the brittle
grass

But there are
on second look
a few yellow leaves
still shaking

far apart

just one here one there
trembling vividly

Portrait of a Lady

Your thighs are appletrees
whose blossoms touch the sky.
Which sky? The sky
where Watteau hung a lady's
slipper. Your knees
are a southern breeze—or
a gust of snow. Agh! what
sort of man was Fragonard?
—as if that answered
anything. Ah, yes—below
the knees, since the tune
drops that way, it is
one of those white summer days,
the tall grass of your ankles
flickers upon the shore—
Which shore?—
the sand clings to my lips—
Which shore?
Agh, petals maybe. How
should I know?
Which shore? Which shore?
I said petals from an appletree.

The Sea-Elephant

Trundled from
the strangeness of the sea—
a kind of
heaven—

Ladies and Gentlemen!
the greatest
sea-monster ever exhibited
alive

the gigantic
sea-elephant! O wallow
of flesh where
are

there fish enough for
that
appetite stupidity
cannot lessen?

Sick
of April's smallness
the little
leaves—

Flesh has lief of you
enormous sea—
Speak!
Blouaugh! (feed

me) my
flesh is riven—

fish after fish into his maw
unswallowing

to let them glide down
gulching back
half spittle half
brine

the
troubled eyes—torn
from the sea.
(In

a practical voice) They
ought
to put it back where
it came from.

Gape.
Strange head—
told by old sailors—
rising

bearded
to the surface—and
the only
sense out of them

is that woman's
Yes
it's wonderful but they
ought to

put it
back into the sea where

it came from.
Blouaugh!

Swing—ride
walk
on wires—toss balls
stoop and

contort yourselves—
But I
am love. I am
from the sea—

Blouaugh!
there is no crime save
the too-heavy
body

the sea
held playfully—comes
to the surface
the water

boiling
about the head the cows
scattering
fish dripping from

the bounty
of . . . . and spring
they say
Spring is icummen in—

Young Sycamore

    I must tell you
this young tree
whose round and firm trunk
between the wet

pavement and the gutter
(where water
is trickling) rises
bodily

into the air with
one undulant
thrust half its height—
and then

dividing and waning
sending out
young branches on
all sides—

hung with cocoons
it thins
till nothing is left of it
but two

eccentric knotted
twigs
bending forward
hornlike at the top

Rain

        As the rain falls
        so does
            your love

        bathe every
            open
        object of the world—

        In houses
        the priceless dry
                rooms
        of illicit love
        where we live
        hear the wash of the
                rain—

        There
            paintings
        and fine
            metalware
        woven stuffs—
        all the whorishness
        of our
            delight
        sees
        from its window

        the spring wash
        of your love
                the falling
        rain—

        The trees
        are become

beasts fresh-risen
from the sea—
water

trickles
from the crevices of
their hides—

So my life is spent
               to keep out love
with which
she rains upon

            the world

of spring

        drips

so spreads

          the words

far apart to let in

             her love

And running in between

the drops

        the rain

is a kind physician

             the rain
of her thoughts over

      the ocean
           every

where

      walking with
invisible swift feet
over

      the helpless
           waves—

Unworldly love
that has no hope
           of the world

           and that
cannot change the world
to its delight—

The rain
falls upon the earth
and grass and flowers

come
      perfectly

into form from its
           liquid

clearness

      But love is
unworldly

      and nothing
comes of it but love

following
and falling endlessly
from
    her thoughts

All the Fancy Things

music and painting and all that
That's all they thought of
in Puerto Rico in the old Spanish
days when she was a girl

So that now
she doesn't know what to do

with herself alone
and growing old up here—

Green is green
but the tag ends
of older things, *ma chère*

must withstand rebuffs
from that which returns
to the beginnings—

Or what? a
clean air, high up, unoffended
by gross odors

Death

He's dead
the dog won't have to
sleep on his potatoes
any more to keep them
from freezing

he's dead
the old bastard—
He's a bastard because

there's nothing
legitimate in him any
more
      he's dead
He's sick-dead

            he's
a godforsaken curio
without
any breath in it

He's nothing at all
      he's dead
shrunken up to skin

      Put his head on
one chair and his
feet on another and
he'll lie there
like an acrobat—

Love's beaten. He
beat it. That's why
he's insufferable—

       because
he's here needing a
shave and making love
an inside howl
of anguish and defeat—

He's come out of the man
and he's let
the man go—
            the liar

Dead
    his eyes
rolled up out of
the light—a mockery

                which
love cannot touch—

just bury it
and hide its face
for shame.

The Red Lily

To the bob-white's call
and drone of reaper

tumbling daisies in the sun—
one by one

about the smutting panels of
white doors

grey shingles slip and fall—
But you, a loveliness

of even lines
curving to the throat, the

crossroads is your home.
You are, upon

your steady stem
one trumpeted wide flower

slightly tilted
above a scale of buds—

Sometimes a farmer's wife
gathers an armful

for her pitcher on the porch—
Topping a stone wall

against the shale-ledge
a field full—

By the road, the river
the edge of the woods

—opening in the sun
closing with the dark—

everywhere
Red Lily

in your common cup
all beauty lies—

The Attic Which Is Desire

        the unused tent
        of

        bare beams
        beyond which

        directly wait
        the night

        and day—
        Here

        from the street
        by

```
* * *
* S *
* O *
* D *
* A *
* * *
```

        ringed with
        running lights

        the darkened
        pane

        exactly
        down the center

        is
        transfixed

The Botticellian Trees

The alphabet of
the trees

is fading in the
song of the leaves

the crossing
bars of the thin

letters that spelled
winter

and the cold
have been illumined

with
pointed green

by the rain and sun—
The strict simple

principles of
straight branches

are being modified
by pinched-out

ifs of color, devout
conditions

the smiles of love—
. . . . . .

until the stript
sentences

move as a woman's
limbs under cloth

and praise from secrecy
quick with desire

love's ascendancy
in summer—

In summer the song
sings itself

above the muffled words—

Nantucket

Flowers through the window
lavender and yellow

changed by white curtains—
Smell of cleanliness—

Sunshine of late afternoon—
On the glass tray

a glass pitcher, the tumbler
turned down, by which

a key is lying—And the
immaculate white bed

The Cod Head

Miscellaneous weed
strands, stems, debris—
firmament

to fishes—
where the yellow feet
of gulls dabble

oars whip
ships churn to bubbles—
at night wildly

agitate phospores-
cent midges—but by day
flaccid

moons in whose
discs sometimes a red cross
lives—four

fathom—the bottom skids
a mottle of green
sands backward—

amorphous waver-
ing rocks—three fathom
the vitreous

body through which—
small scudding fish deep
down—and

> now a lulling lift
> and fall—
> red stars—a severed cod—
>
> head between two
> green stones—lifting
> falling

To Mark Anthony in Heaven

> This quiet morning light
> reflected, how many times
> from grass and trees and clouds
> enters my north room
> touching the walls with
> grass and clouds and trees.
> Anthony,
> trees and grass and clouds.
> Why did you follow
> that beloved body
> with your ships at Actium?
> I hope it was because
> you knew her inch by inch
> from slanting feet upward
> to the roots of her hair
> and down again and that
> you saw her
> above the battle's fury—
> clouds and trees and grass—
>
> For then you are
> listening in heaven.

The Bull

        It is in captivity—
        ringed, haltered, chained
        to a drag
        the bull is godlike

        Unlike the cows
        he lives alone, nozzles
        the sweet grass gingerly
        to pass the time away

        He kneels, lies down
        and stretching out
        a foreleg licks himself
        about the hoof

        then stays
        with half-closed eyes,
        Olympian commentary on
        the bright passage of days.

        —The round sun
        smooth his lacquer
        through
        the glossy pinetrees

        his substance hard
        as ivory or glass—
        through which the wind
        yet plays—
                      milkless

he nods
the hair between his horns
and eyes matted
with hyacinthine curls

The Lily

The branching head of
tiger-lilies through the window
in the air—

A humming bird
is still on whirring wings
above the flowers—

By spotted petals curling back
and tongues that hang
the air is seen—

It's raining—
water's caught
among the curled-back petals

Caught and held
and there's a fly—
are blossoming

Poem

>As the cat
>climbed over
>the top of
>
>the jamcloset
>first the right
>forefoot
>
>carefully
>then the hind
>stepped down
>
>into the pit of
>the empty
>flowerpot

On Gay Wallpaper

>The green-blue ground
>is ruled with silver lines
>to say the sun is shining
>
>And on this moral sea
>of grass or dreams lie flowers
>or baskets of desires
>
>Heaven knows what they are
>between cerulean shapes
>laid regularly round

Mat roses and tridentate
leaves of gold
threes, threes and threes

Three roses and three stems
the basket floating
standing in the horns of blue

Repeated to the ceiling
to the windows
where the day

Blows in
the scalloped curtains to
the sound of rain

This Is Just to Say

        I have eaten
        the plums
        that were in
        the icebox

        and which
        you were probably
        saving
        for breakfast

        Forgive me
        they were delicious
        so sweet
        and so cold

It Is a Living Coral

a trouble

archaically fettered
to produce

E Pluribus Unum an
island

in the sea a Capitol
surmounted

by Armed Liberty—
painting

sculpture straddled by
a dome

eight million pounds
in weight

iron plates constructed
to expand

and contract with
variations

of temperature
the folding

and unfolding of a lily.
And Congress

authorized and the
Commission

was entrusted was
entrusted!

a sculptured group
Mars

in Roman mail placing
a wreath

of laurel on the brow
of Washington

Commerce Minerva
Thomas

Jefferson John Hancock
at

the table Mrs. Motte
presenting

Indian burning arrows
to Generals

Marion and Lee to fire
her mansion

and dislodge the British—
this scaleless

jumble is superb

and accurate in its
expression

of the thing they
would destroy—

Baptism of Poca-
hontas

with a little card
hanging

under it to tell
the persons

in the picture.

It climbs

it runs, it is Geo.
Shoup

of Idaho it wears
a beard

it fetches naked
Indian

women from a river
Trumbull

Varnum Henderson
Frances

Willard's corset is
absurd—

Banks White Columbus
stretched

in bed men felling trees

The Hon. Michael
C. Kerr

onetime Speaker of
the House

of Representatives
Perry

in a rowboat on Lake
Erie

changing ships the
dead

among the wreckage
sickly green

The Trees

The trees—being trees
thrash and scream
guffaw and curse—
wholly abandoned
damning the race of men—

Christ, the bastards
haven't even sense enough
to stay out in the rain—

Wha ha ha ha

Wheeeeee
Clacka tacka tacka
tacka tacka
wha ha ha ha ha
ha ha ha

knocking knees, buds
bursting from each pore
even the trunk's self
putting out leafheads—

Loose desire!
we naked cry to you—
"Do what you please."

You cannot!

—ghosts
sapped of strength

wailing at the gate
heartbreak at the bridgehead—

desire
dead in the heart

haw haw haw haw
—and memory broken

wheeeeee

There were never satyrs
never maenads
never eagle-headed gods—
These were men
from whose hands sprung
love

bursting the wood—
Trees their companions
—a cold wind winterlong
in the hollows of our flesh
icy with pleasure—

no part of us untouched

The Catholic Bells

Tho' I'm no Catholic
I listen hard when the bells
in the yellow-brick tower
of their new church

ring down the leaves
ring in the frost upon them
and the death of the flowers
ring out the grackle

toward the south, the sky
darkened by them, ring in
the new baby of Mr. and Mrs.
Krantz which cannot

for the fat of its cheeks
open well its eyes, ring out
the parrot under its hood
jealous of the child

ring in Sunday morning
and old age which adds as it
takes away. Let them ring
only ring! over the oil

painting of a young priest
on the church wall advertising
last week's Novena to St.
Anthony, ring for the lame

young man in black with
gaunt cheeks and wearing a
Derby hat, who is hurrying
to 11 o'clock Mass (the

grapes still hanging to
the vine along the nearby
Concordia Halle like broken
teeth in the head of an

old man) Let them ring
for the eyes and ring for
the hands and ring for
the children of my friend

who no longer hears
them ring but with a smile
and in a low voice speaks
of the decisions of her

daughter and the proposals
and betrayals of her
husband's friends. O bells
ring for the ringing!

the beginning and the end
of the ringing! Ring ring
ring ring ring ring ring!
Catholic bells—!

Flowers by the Sea

When over the flowery, sharp pasture's
edge, unseen, the salt ocean

lifts its form—chicory and daisies
tied, released, seem hardly flowers alone

but color and the movement—or the shape
perhaps—of restlessness, whereas

the sea is circled and sways
peacefully upon its plantlike stem

Proletarian Portrait

A big young bareheaded woman
in an apron

Her hair slicked back standing
on the street

One stockinged foot toeing
the sidewalk

Her shoe in her hand. Looking
intently into it

She pulls out the paper insole
to find the nail

That has been hurting her

An Elegy for D. H. Lawrence

Green points on the shrub
and poor Lawrence dead.
The night damp and misty
and Lawrence no more in the world
to answer April's promise
with a fury of labor
against waste, waste and life's
coldness.

Once he received a letter—
he never answered it—
praising him: so English
he had thereby raised himself
to an unenglish greatness.
Dead now and it grows clearer
what bitterness drove him.

This is the time.
The serpent in the grotto
water dripping from the stone
into a pool.
Mediterranean evenings. Ashes
of Cretan fires. And to the north
forsythia hung with
yellow bells in the cold.

Poor Lawrence
worn with a fury of sad labor
to create summer from
spring's decay. English
women. Men driven not to love
but to the ends of the earth.
The serpent turning his

stone-like head,
the fixed agate eyes turn also.

And unopened jonquils
hang their folded heads. No
summer. But for Lawrence
full praise in this
half cold half season—
before trees are in leaf and
tufted grass stars
unevenly the bare ground.

Slowly the serpent leans
to drink by the tinkling water
the forked tongue alert,
Then fold after fold,
glassy strength, passing
a given point,
as by desire drawn
forward bodily, he glides
smoothly in.

To stand by the sea or walk
again along a river's bank and talk
with a companion, to halt
watching where the edge of water
meets and lies upon
the unmoving shore—
Flood waters rise, and will rise,
rip the quiet valley
trap the gypsy and the girl
She clings drowning to
a bush in flower.

Remember, now, Lawrence dead.
Blue squills in bloom—to
the scorched aridity of

the Mexican plateau. Or baked
public squares in the cities of
Mediterranean islands
where one waits for busses and
boats come slowly along the water
arriving.

But the sweep of spring over
temperate lands, meadows and woods
where the young walk and talk
incompletely,
straining to no summer,
hearing the frogs, speaking of
birds and insects—

Febrile spring moves not to heat
but always more slowly,
burdened by a weight of leaves.
Nothing now
to burst the bounds—
remains confined by them. Heat,
heat! Unknown. Poor Lawrence,
dead and only the drowned
fallen dancing from the deck
of a pleasure boat
unfading desire.

Rabbits, imaginings, the
drama, literature, satire.
The serpent cannot move
his stony eyes, scarcely sees
but touching the air
with his forked tongue surmises
and his body which dipped
into the cold water
is gone.

Violently the satiric sun
that leads April not to
the panting dance but to stillness
in, into the brain, dips
and is gone also.
And sisters return
through the dusk
to the measured rancor
of their unbending elders.

Greep, greep, greep the cricket
chants where the snake
with agate eyes leaned to the water.
Sorrow to the young
that Lawrence has passed
unwanted from England.
And in the gardens forsythia
and in the woods
now the crinkled spice-bush
in flower.

To a Poor Old Woman

      munching a plum on
      the street a paper bag
      of them in her hand

      They taste good to her
      They taste good
      to her. They taste
      good to her

You can see it by
the way she gives herself
to the one half
sucked out in her hand

Comforted
a solace of ripe plums
seeming to fill the air
They taste good to her

The Locust Tree in Flower

      Among
      of
      green

      stiff
      old
      bright

      broken
      branch
      come

      white
      sweet
      May

      again

The Wind Increases

       The harried
       earth is swept
                The trees
       the tulip's bright
           tips
                sidle and
  toss—

         Loose your love
  to flow

  Blow!

  Good Christ what is
  a poet—if any
               exists?

  a man
  whose words will
       bite
             their way
  home—being actual

  having the form
             of motion

  At each twigtip

  new

  upon the tortured
  body of thought

>   gripping
>   the ground
>
>   a way
>   to the last leaftip

Fine Work with Pitch and Copper

>   Now they are resting
>   in the fleckless light
>   separately in unison
>
>   like the sacks
>   of sifted stone stacked
>   regularly by twos
>
>   about the flat roof
>   ready after lunch
>   to be opened and strewn
>
>   The copper in eight
>   foot strips has been
>   beaten lengthwise
>
>   down the center at right
>   angles and lies ready
>   to edge the coping
>
>   One still chewing
>   picks up a copper strip
>   and runs his eye along it

The Yachts

contend in a sea which the land partly encloses
shielding them from the too-heavy blows
of an ungoverned ocean which when it chooses

tortures the biggest hulls, the best man knows
to pit against its beatings, and sinks them pitilessly.
Mothlike in mists, scintillant in the minute

brilliance of cloudless days, with broad bellying sails
they glide to the wind tossing green water
from their sharp prows while over them the crew crawls

ant-like, solicitously grooming them, releasing,
making fast as they turn, lean far over and having
caught the wind again, side by side, head for the mark.

In a well guarded arena of open water surrounded by
lesser and greater craft which, sycophant, lumbering
and flittering follow them, they appear youthful, rare

as the light of a happy eye, live with the grace
of all that in the mind is fleckless, free and
naturally to be desired. Now the sea which holds them

is moody, lapping their glossy sides, as if feeling
for some slightest flaw but fails completely.
Today no race. Then the wind comes again. The yachts

move, jockeying for a start, the signal is set and they
are off. Now the waves strike at them but they are too
well made, they slip through, though they take in canvas.

Arms with hands grasping seek to clutch at the prows.
Bodies thrown recklessly in the way are cut aside.
It is a sea of faces about them in agony, in despair

until the horror of the race dawns staggering the mind;
the whole sea become an entanglement of watery bodies
lost to the world bearing what they cannot hold. Broken,

beaten, desolate, reaching from the dead to be taken up
they cry out, failing, failing! their cries rising
in waves still as the skillful yachts pass over.

Adam

>He grew up by the sea
>on a hot island
>inhabited by negroes—mostly.
>There he built himself
>a boat and a separate room
>close to the water
>for a piano on which he practiced—
>by sheer doggedness
>and strength of purpose
>striving
>like an Englishman
>to emulate his Spanish friend
>and idol—the weather!
>
>And there he learned
>to play the flute—not very well—

Thence he was driven
out of Paradise—to taste
the death that duty brings
so daintily, so mincingly,
with such a noble air—
that enslaved him all his life
thereafter—

And he left behind
all the curious memories that come
with shells and hurricanes—
the smells
and sounds and glancing looks
that Latins know belong
to boredom and long torrid hours
and Englishmen
will never understand—whom
duty has marked
for special mention—with
a tropic of its own
and its own heavy-winged fowl
and flowers that vomit beauty
at midnight—

But the Latin has turned romance
to a purpose cold as ice.
He never sees
or seldom
what melted Adam's knees
to jelly and despair—and
held them up pontifically—

Underneath the whisperings
of tropic nights
there is a darker whispering

that death invents especially
for northern men
whom the tropics
have come to hold.

It would have been enough
to know that never,
never, never, never would
peace come as the sun comes
in the hot islands.
But there was
a special hell besides
where black women lie waiting
for a boy—

Naked on a raft
he could see the barracudas
waiting to castrate him
so the saying went—
Circumstances take longer—

But being an Englishman
though he had not lived in England
desde que avia cinco años
he never turned back
but kept a cold eye always
on the inevitable end
never wincing—never to unbend—
God's handyman
going quietly into hell's mouth
for a paper of reference—
fetching water to posterity
a British passport
always in his pocket—
muleback over Costa Rica
eating pâtés of black ants

And the Latin ladies admired him
and under their smiles
dartled the dagger of despair—
in spite of
a most thorough trial—
found his English heart safe
in the roseate steel. Duty
the angel
which with whip in hand . . .
—along the low wall of paradise
where they sat and smiled
and flipped their fans
at him—

He never had but the one home
Staring Him in the eye
coldly
and with patience—
without a murmur, silently
a desperate, unvarying silence
to the unhurried last.

St. Francis Einstein of the Daffodils

*On the first visit of Professor Einstein to
the United States in the spring of 1921.*

"Sweet land"
at last!
out of the sea—
the Venusremembering wavelets
rippling with laughter—
freedom
for the daffodils!

—in a tearing wind
that shakes
the tufted orchards—
Einstein, tall as a violet
in the lattice-arbor corner
is tall as
a blossomy peartree

A Samos, Samos
dead and buried. Lesbia
a black cat in the freshturned
garden. All dead.
All flesh they sung
is rotten
Sing of it no longer—

Side by side young and old
take the sun together—
maples, green and red
yellowbells
and the vermilion quinceflower
together—

The peartree
with fœtid blossoms
sways its high topbranches
with contrary motions
and there are both pinkflowered
and coralflowered peachtrees
in the bare chickenyard
of the old negro
with white hair who hides
poisoned fish-heads
here and there
where stray cats find them—
find them

Spring days
swift and mutable
winds blowing four ways
hot and cold
shaking the flowers—

Now the northeast wind
moving in fogs leaves the grass
cold and dripping. The night
is dark. But in the night
the southeast wind approaches.
The owner of the orchard
lies in bed
with open windows
and throws off his covers
one by one

The Young Housewife

At ten A.M. the young housewife
moves about in negligee behind
the wooden walls of her husband's house.
I pass solitary in my car.

Then again she comes to the curb
to call the ice-man, fish-man, and stands
shy, uncorseted, tucking in
stray ends of hair, and I compare her
to a fallen leaf.

The noiseless wheels of my car
rush with a crackling sound over
dried leaves as I bow and pass smiling.

Perpetuum Mobile: The City

          —a dream
      we dreamed
         each
    separately
       we two

of love
      and of
desire—

that fused
in the night—

in the distance
     over
the meadows
    by day
impossible—
    The city
disappeared
    when
we arrived—

    A dream
a little false

toward which
    now
we stand
    and stare
transfixed—

All at once
          in the east
rising!

          All white!

          small
as a flower—

a locust cluster
a shad bush
          blossoming

Over the swamps
          a wild
magnolia bud—
          greenish
white
a northern
          flower—
And so
          we live
          looking—

At night
          it wakes
On the black
          sky—

a dream
          toward which
we love—
at night
          more
than a little
          false—

We have bred
we have dug
we have figured up
our costs
we have bought
an old rug—

We batter at our
unsatisfactory
        brilliance—

There is no end
        to desire—

Let us break
        through
and go there—

in
        vain!

—delectable
        amusement:

Milling about—

Money! in
armored trucks—
Two men
        walking
at two paces from
        each other
their right hands
        at the hip—
on the butt of
an automatic—

till they themselves
hold up the bank
and themselves
    drive off
for themselves
    the money
in an armored car—

For love!

Carefully
    carefully tying
carefully

    selected
wisps of long
dark hair
    wisp
by wisp
upon the stubs
of his kinky wool—
For two hours
    they worked—
    until
he coiled
    the thick
knot upon
that whorish
    head—

Dragged
    insensible
upon his face
by the lines—

—a running horse

For love.

Their eyes
         blown out—

—for love, for love!

Neither the rain
Nor the storm—
can keep them

         for love!

from the daily
accomplishment
      of their
appointed rounds—

Guzzling
the creamy foods
         while
out of sight
         in
the sub-cellar—
the waste fat
the old vegetables
         chucked down
a chute
         the foulest
sink in the world—

And go
on the out-tide
ten thousands
         cots
floating to sea

                    like weed
            that held back
            the pristine ships—

            And fattened there
            an eel
            in the water pipe—

                    No end—

            There!

                    There!

            There!

                    —a dream
            of lights
                    hiding

            the iron reason
                    and stone
            a settled
                    cloud—

            City

                    whose stars
            of matchless
                    splendor—

                    and
            in bright-edged
                    clouds
            the moon—

                    bring

        silence

                    breathlessly—

Tearful city
            on a summer's day
the hard grey
            dwindling
in a wall of
            rain—

                    farewell!

Between Walls

                the back wings
                of the

                hospital where
                nothing

                will grow lie
                cinders

                in which shine
                the broken

                pieces of a green
                bottle

Paterson: Episode 17

Beat hell out of it
  Beautiful Thing
  spotless cap
and crossed white straps
over the dark rippled cloth—
  Lift the stick
above that easy head
where you sit by the ivied
church, one arm
  buttressing you
long fingers spread out
among the clear grass prongs—
  and drive it down
  Beautiful Thing
that your caressing body kiss
  and kiss again
that holy lawn—

And again: obliquely—
legs curled under you as a
  deer's leaping—
pose of supreme indifference
  sacrament
to a summer's day
  Beautiful Thing
in the unearned suburbs
  then pause
  the arm fallen—
what memories
of what forgotten face
brooding upon that lily stem?

    The incredible
nose straight from the brow
  the empurpled lips
and dazzled half-sleepy eyes
  Beautiful Thing
of some trusting animal
  makes a temple
of its place of savage slaughter
  revealing
the damaged will incites still
  to violence
consummately beautiful thing
and falls about your resting
  shoulders—

Gently! Gently!
as in all things an opposite
  that awakes
the fury, conceiving
  knowledge
by way of despair that has
  no place
to lay its glossy head—
Save only—Not alone!
  Never, if possible
alone! to escape the accepted
  chopping block
and a square hat!—

And as reverie gains and
  your joints loosen
  the trick's done!
Day is covered and we see you—
  but not alone!
drunk and bedraggled to release
the strictness of beauty

under a sky full of stars
   Beautiful Thing
and a slow moon—
                    The car
   had stopped long since
   when the others
came and dragged those out
   who had you there
   indifferent
to whatever the anesthetic
   Beautiful Thing
might slum away the bars—
Reek of it!
   What does it matter?
   could set free
only the one thing—
But you!
—in your white lace dress
   "the dying swan"
and high heeled slippers—tall
as you already were—
   till your head
through fruitful exaggeration
was reaching the sky and the
prickles of its ecstasy
   Beautiful Thing!

And the guys from Paterson
   beat up
the guys from Newark and told
them to stay the hell out
of their territory and then
socked you one
   across the nose
   Beautiful Thing
for good luck and emphasis

   cracking it
till I must believe that all
desired women have had each
 in the end
 a busted nose
and live afterward marked up
 Beautiful Thing
 for memory's sake
to be credible in their deeds

Then back to the party!
 and they maled
and femaled you jealously
 Beautiful Thing
as if to discover when and
 by what miracle
there should escape what?
still to be possessed
out of what part
 Beautiful Thing
should it look?
 or be extinguished—
Three days in the same dress
 up and down—
 It would take
a Dominie to be patient
 Beautiful Thing
with you—

The stroke begins again—
 regularly
automatic
 contrapuntal to
the flogging
like the beat of famous lines
in the few excellent poems

>   woven to make you
>   gracious
>   and on frequent occasions
>   foul drunk
>   Beautiful Thing
>   pulse of release
>   to the attentive
>   and obedient mind.

A Coronal

New books of poetry will be written
New books and unheard of manuscripts
will come wrapped in brown paper
and many and many a time
the postman will blow
and sidle down the leaf-plastered steps
thumbing over other men's business

But we ran ahead of it all.
One coming after
could have seen her footprints
in the wet and followed us
among the stark chestnuts.

Anemones sprang where she pressed
and cresses
stood green in the slender source—
And new books of poetry
will be written, leather-colored oakleaves
many and many a time.

These

       are the desolate, dark weeks
       when nature in its barrenness
       equals the stupidity of man.

       The year plunges into night
       and the heart plunges
       lower than night

       to an empty, windswept place
       without sun, stars or moon
       but a peculiar light as of thought

       that spins a dark fire—
       whirling upon itself until,
       in the cold, it kindles

       to make a man aware of nothing
       that he knows, not loneliness
       itself—Not a ghost but

       would be embraced—emptiness,
       despair—(They
       whine and whistle) among

       the flashes and booms of war;
       houses of whose rooms
       the cold is greater than can be thought,

       the people gone that we loved,
       the beds lying empty, the couches
       damp, the chairs unused—

Hide it away somewhere
out of the mind, let it get roots
and grow, unrelated to jealous

ears and eyes—for itself.
In this mine they come to dig—all.
Is this the counterfoil to sweetest

music? The source of poetry that
seeing the clock stopped, says,
The clock has stopped

that ticked yesterday so well?
and hears the sound of lakewater
splashing—that is now stone.

The Term

                A rumpled sheet
                of brown paper
                about the length

                and apparent bulk
                of a man was
                rolling with the

                wind slowly over
                and over in
                the street as

                a car drove down
                upon it and
                crushed it to

the ground. Unlike
a man it rose
again rolling

with the wind over
and over to be as
it was before.

The Poor

It's the anarchy of poverty
delights me, the old
yellow wooden house indented
among the new brick tenements

Or a cast-iron balcony
with panels showing oak branches
in full leaf. It fits
the dress of the children

reflecting every stage and
custom of necessity—
Chimneys, roofs, fences of
wood and metal in an unfenced

age and enclosing next to
nothing at all: the old man
in a sweater and soft black
hat who sweeps the sidewalk—

his own ten feet of it
in a wind that fitfully
turning his corner has
overwhelmed the entire city

A Marriage Ritual

                      Above
the darkness of a river upon
winter's icy sky
dreams the silhouette of the city:

This is my own! a flower,
a fruit, an animal by itself—

It does not recognize me
and never will. Still, it is my own
and my heart goes out to it
dumbly—

    but eloquently in
my own breast for you whom I love
—and cannot express what
my love is, how it varies, though
I waste it—

      It is
a river flowing through refuse
the dried sticks of weeds
and falling shell-ice lilac
from above as if with thoughts
of you—

This is my face and its moods
my moods, a riffled whiteness
shaken by the flow
that's constant in its swiftness
as a pool—

          A Polack in
the stinging wind, her arms
wrapped to her breast
comes shambling near. To look
at what? downstream. It is
an old-world flavor: the poor
the unthrifty, passionately biased
by what errors of conviction—

          Now a boy
is rolling a stout metal drum
up from below the river bank.
The woman and the boy, two
thievish figures, struggle with
the object.... in this light!

                And still
there is one leafless tree
just at the water's edge and—

                      my face
constant to you!

The Last Words of My English Grandmother

1920

There were some dirty plates
and a glass of milk
beside her on a small table
near the rank, disheveled bed—

Wrinkled and nearly blind
she lay and snored
rousing with anger in her tones
to cry for food,

Gimme something to eat—
They're starving me—
I'm all right I won't go
to the hospital. No, no, no

Give me something to eat
Let me take you
to the hospital, I said
and after you are well

you can do as you please.
She smiled, Yes
you do what you please first
then I can do what I please—

Oh, oh, oh! she cried
as the ambulance men lifted
her to the stretcher—
Is this what you call

making me comfortable?
By now her mind was clear—
Oh you think you're smart
you young people,

she said, but I'll tell you
you don't know anything.
Then we started.
On the way

we passed a long row
of elms. She looked at them
awhile out of
the ambulance window and said,

What are all those
fuzzy-looking things out there?
Trees? Well, I'm tired
of them and rolled her head away.

Impromptu: The Suckers

Take it out in vile whisky, take it out
in lifting your skirts to show your silken
crotches; it is this that is intended.
You are it. Your pleas will always be denied.
You too will always go up with the two guys,
scapegoats to save the Republic and
especially the State of Massachusetts. The
Governor says so and you ain't supposed
to ask for details—

Your case has been reviewed by high-minded
and unprejudiced observers (like hell
they were!) the president of a great
university, the president of a noteworthy
technical school and a judge too old to sit
on the bench, men already rewarded for
their services to pedagogy and the enforcement
of arbitrary statutes. In other words
pimps to tradition—

Why in hell didn't they choose some other
kind of "unprejudiced adviser" for their
death council? instead of sticking to that
autocratic strain of Boston backwash, except

that the council was far from unprejudiced
but the product of a rejected, discredited
class long since outgrown except for use in
courts and school, and that they
wanted it so—

Why didn't they choose at least one decent
Jew or some fair-minded Negro or anybody
but such a triumvirate of inversion, the
New England aristocracy, bent on working off
a grudge against you, Americans, you
are the suckers, you are the ones who will
be going up on the eleventh to get the current
shot into you, for the glory of the state
and the perpetuation of abstract justice—

And all this in the face of the facts: that
the man who swore, and deceived the jury
wilfully by so doing, that the bullets found
in the bodies of the deceased could be
identified as having been fired from the pistol
of one of the accused—later
acknowledged that he could not so identify
them; that the jurors now seven years after
the crime do not remember the details and
have wanted to forget them; that the
prosecution has never succeeded in
apprehending the accomplices nor in connecting
the prisoners with any of the loot stolen—

The case is perfect against you, all the
documents say so—in spite of the fact that
it is reasonably certain that you were not
at the scene of the crime, shown, quite as
convincingly as the accusing facts in the
court evidence, by better reasoning to have

been committed by someone else with whom
the loot can be connected and among whom the
accomplices can be found—

It's no use, you are Americans, just the dregs.
It's all you deserve. You've got the cash,
what the hell do you care? You've got
nothing to lose. You are inheritors of a great
tradition. My country right or wrong!
You do what you're told to do. You don't
answer back the way Tommy Jeff did or Ben
Frank or Georgie Washing. I'll say you
don't. You're civilized. You let your
betters tell you where you get off. Go
ahead—

But after all, the thing that swung heaviest
against you was that you were scared when
they copped you. Explain that you
nature's nobleman! For you know that every
American is innocent and at peace in his
own heart. He hasn't a damned thing to be
afraid of. He knows the government is for
him. Why, when a cop steps up and grabs
you at night you just laugh and think it's
a hell of a good joke—

This is what was intended from the first.
So take it out in your rotten whisky and
silk underwear. That's what you get out of
it. But put it down in your memory that this
is the kind of stuff that they can't get away
with. It is there and it's loaded. No one
can understand what makes the present age
what it is. They are mystified by certain
insistences.

Raleigh Was Right

    We cannot go to the country
    for the country will bring us
        no peace
    What can the small violets tell us
    that grow on furry stems in
    the long grass among lance shaped
        leaves?

    Though you praise us
    and call to mind the poets
    who sung of our loveliness
    it was long ago!
    long ago! when country people
    would plow and sow with
    flowering minds and pockets
        at ease—
    if ever this were true.

    Not now. Love itself a flower
    with roots in a parched ground.
    Empty pockets make empty heads.
    Cure it if you can but
    do not believe that we can live
    today in the country
    for the country will bring us
        no peace.

The Clouds

I

Filling the mind
upon the rim of the overarching sky, the
    horses of
the dawn charge from south to north,
    gigantic beasts
rearing flame-edged above the pit,
a rank confusion of the imagination still
    uncured
a rule, piebald under the streetlamps,
    reluctant
to be torn from its hold.

                  Their flanks still
caught among low, blocking forms their
    fore-parts
rise lucid beyond this smell of a swamp, a mud
livid with decay and life! turtles
that burrowing among the white roots lift
    their green
red-striped faces startled before the dawn.

A black flag, writhing and whipping at the
    staff-head
mounts the sepulcher of the empty bank,
    fights
to be free . . .
            South to north! the direction
unmistakable, they move, distinct beyond
    the unclear
edge of the world, clouds! like statues
before which we are drawn—in darkness,

           thinking of
our dead, unable, knowing no place
where else rightly to lodge them.

                         Tragic outlines
and the bodies of horses, mindfilling—but
visible! against the invisible; actual against
the imagined and the concocted; unspoiled
    by hands
and unshaped also by them but caressed by
    sight only,
moving among them, not that that propels
the eyes from under, while it blinds:

—upon whose backs the dead ride, high!
undirtied by the putridity we fasten upon
    them—
South to north, for this moment distinct
    and undeformed,
into the no-knowledge of their nameless
    destiny.

II

Where are the good minds of past days, the unshorn?
Villon, to be sure, with his
saw-toothed will and testament? Erasmus
who praised folly and

Shakespeare who wrote so that
no school man or churchman could sanction him without
revealing his own imbecility? Aristotle,
shrewd and alone, a onetime herb peddler?

They all, like Aristophanes, knew the clouds and
said next to nothing of the soul's flight
but kept their heads and died—
like Socrates, Plato's better self, unmoved.

Where? They live today in their old state because
of the pace they kept that keeps
them now fresh in our thoughts, their
relics, ourselves: Toulouse-Lautrec, the

deformed who lived in a brothel and painted
the beauty of whores. These were
the truth-tellers of whom we are the sole heirs
beneath the clouds that bring

shadow and darkness full of thought deepened
by rain against the clatter
of an empty sky. But anything to escape humanity!
Now it's spiritualism—again,

as if the certainty of a future life
were any solution to our dilemma: how to get
published not what we write but what we would write were
it not for the laws against libelous truth.

The poor brain unwilling to own the obtrusive body
would crawl from it like a crab and
because it succeeds, at times, in doffing that,
by its wiles of drugs or other "ecstasies," thinks

at last that it is quite free—exulted, scurrying to
some slightly larger shell some snail
has lost (where it will live). And so, thinking,
pretends a mystery! an unbodied

thing that would still be a brain—but no body,
something that does not eat but flies by the propulsions
of pure—what? into the sun itself, illimitedly
and exists so forever, blest, washed, purged

and at ease in non-representational bursts
of shapeless flame, sentient (naturally!)—and keeps
touch with the earth (by former works) at least.
The intellect leads, leads still! Beyond the clouds.

III

(Scherzo)

I came upon a priest once at St. Andrew's
in Amalfi in crimson and gold brocade riding
the clouds of his belief.

It happened that we tourists had intervened
at some mid-moment of the ritual—
tipped the sacristan or whatever it was.

No one else was there—porphyry and alabaster,
the light flooding in scented
with sandalwood—but this holy man

jiggling upon his buttocks to the litany
chanted, in response, by two kneeling altar boys!
I was amazed and stared in such manner

that he, caught half off the earth
in his ecstasy—though without losing a beat—
turned and grinned at me from his cloud.

IV

With each, dies a piece of the old life, which he carries,
a precious burden, beyond! Thus each
is valued by what he carries and that is his soul—
diminishing the bins by that much
unless replenished.

              It is that which is the brotherhood:
the old life, treasured. But if they live?
What then?

            The clouds remain
—the disordered heavens, ragged, ripped by winds
or dormant, a caligraphy of scaly dragons and bright moths,
of straining thought, bulbous or smooth,
ornate, the flesh itself (in which
the poet foretells his own death); convoluted, lunging upon
a pismire, a conflagration, a . . . .

The Yellow Chimney

        There is a plume
        of fleshpale
        smoke upon the blue

        sky. The silver
        rings that
        strap the yellow

brick stack at
wide intervals shine
in this amber

light—not
of the sun not of
the pale sun but

his born brother
the
declining season

The Semblables

The red brick monastery in
the suburbs over against the dust-
hung acreage of the unfinished
and all but subterranean

munitions plant: those high
brick walls behind which at Easter
the little orphans and bastards
in white gowns sing their Latin

responses to the hoary ritual
while frankincense and myrrh
round out the dark chapel making
an enclosed sphere of it

of which they are the worm:
that cell outside the city beside
the polluted stream and dump
heap, uncomplaining, and the field

of upended stones with a photo
under glass fastened here and there
to one of them near the deeply
carved name to distinguish it:

that trinity of slate gables
the unembellished windows piling
up, the chapel with its round
window between the dormitories

peaked by the bronze belfry
peaked in turn by the cross,
verdegris—faces all silent
that miracle that has burst sexless

from between the carrot rows.
Leafless white birches, their
empty tendrils swaying in
the all but no breeze guard

behind the spiked monastery fence
the sacred statuary. But ranks
of brilliant car-tops row on row
give back in all his glory the

late November sun and hushed
attend, before that tumbled
ground, those sightless walls
and shovelled entrances where no

one but a lonesome cop swinging
his club gives sign, that agony
within where the wrapt machines
are praying. . . .

To Ford Madox Ford in Heaven

    Is it any better in Heaven, my friend Ford,
        than you found it in Provence?

I don't think so for you made Provence a
        heaven by your praise of it
to give a foretaste of what might be
        your joy in the present circumstances.
It was Heaven you were describing there
        transubstantiated from its narrowness
to resemble the paths and gardens of a
        greater world where you now reside.
But, dear man, you have taken a major
        part of it from us.
                Provence that you
praised so well will never be the same
        Provence to us
                now you are gone.

A heavenly man you seem to me now, never
        having been for me a saintly one.
It lived about you, a certain grossness that
        was not like the world.
The world is cleanly, polished and well
        made but heavenly man
is filthy with his flesh and corrupt that
        loves to eat and drink and whore—
to laugh at himself and not be afraid of
        himself knowing well he has
no possessions and opinions that are worth
        caring a broker's word about
and that all he is, but one thing, he feeds
        as one will feed a pet dog.

So roust and love and dredge the belly full
 in Heaven's name!
I laugh to think of you wheezing in Heaven.
 Where is Heaven? But why
do I ask that, since you showed the way?
 I don't care a damn for it
other than for that better part lives beside
 me here so long as I
live and remember you. Thank God you
 were not delicate, you let the world in
and lied! damn it you lied grossly
 sometimes. But it was all, I
see now, a carelessness, the part of a man
 that is homeless here on earth.

Provence, the fat assed Ford will never
 again strain the chairs of your cafés
pull and pare for his dish your sacred garlic,
 grunt and sweat and lick
his lips. Gross as the world he has left to
 us he has become
a part of that of which you were the known
 part, Provence, he loved so well.

A Sort of a Song

Let the snake wait under
his weed
and the writing
be of words, slow and quick, sharp
to strike, quiet to wait,
sleepless.

—through metaphor to reconcile
the people and the stones.
Compose. (No ideas
but in things) Invent!
Saxifrage is my flower that splits
the rocks.

Burning the Christmas Greens

Their time past, pulled down
cracked and flung to the fire
—go up in a roar

All recognition lost, burnt clean
clean in the flame, the green
dispersed, a living red,
flame red, red as blood wakes
on the ash—

and ebbs to a steady burning
the rekindled bed become
a landscape of flame

At the winter's midnight
we went to the trees, the coarse
holly, the balsam and
the hemlock for their green

At the thick of the dark
the moment of the cold's
deepest plunge we brought branches
cut from the green trees

to fill our need, and over
doorways, about paper Christmas
bells covered with tinfoil
and fastened by red ribbons

we stuck the green prongs
in the windows hung
woven wreaths and above pictures
the living green. On the

mantle we built a green forest
and among those hemlock
sprays put a herd of small
white deer as if they

were walking there. All this!
and it seemed gentle and good
to us. Their time past,
relief! The room bare. We

stuffed the dead grate
with them upon the half burnt out
log's smoldering eye, opening
red and closing under them

and we stood there looking down.
Green is a solace
a promise of peace, a fort
against the cold (though we

did not say so) a challenge
above the snow's
hard shell. Green (we might
have said) that, where

small birds hide and dodge
and lift their plaintive
rallying cries, blocks for them
and knocks down

the unseeing bullets of
the storm. Green spruce boughs
pulled down by a weight of
snow—Transformed!

Violence leaped and appeared.
Recreant! roared to life
as the flame rose through and
our eyes recoiled from it.

In the jagged flames green
to red, instant and alive. Green!
those sure abutments . . . Gone!
lost to mind

and quick in the contracting
tunnel of the grate
appeared a world! Black
mountains, black and red—as

yet uncolored—and ash white,
an infant landscape of shimmering
ash and flame and we, in
that instant, lost,

breathless to be witnesses,
as if we stood
ourselves refreshed among
the shining fauna of that fire.

Paterson: the Falls

What common language to unravel?
The Falls, combed into straight lines
from that rafter of a rock's
lip. Strike in! the middle of

some trenchant phrase, some
well packed clause. Then . . .
This is my plan. 4 sections: First,
the archaic persons of the drama.

An eternity of bird and bush,
resolved. An unraveling:
the confused streams aligned, side
by side, speaking! Sound

married to strength, a strength
of falling—from a height! The wild
voice of the shirt-sleeved
Evangelist rivaling, Hear

me! I am the Resurrection
and the Life! echoing
among the bass and pickerel, slim
eels from Barbados, Sargasso

Sea, working up the coast to that
bounty, ponds and wild streams—
Third, the old town: Alexander Hamilton
working up from St. Croix,

from that sea! and a deeper, whence
he came! stopped cold

by that unmoving roar, fastened
there: the rocks silent

but the water, married to the stone,
voluble, though frozen; the water
even when and though frozen
still whispers and moans—

And in the brittle air
a factory bell clangs, at dawn, and
snow whines under their feet. Fourth,
the modern town, a

disembodied roar! the cataract and
its clamor broken apart—and from
all learning, the empty
ear struck from within, roaring . . .

The Dance

In Breughel's great picture, The Kermess,
the dancers go round, they go round and
around, the squeal and the blare and the
tweedle of bagpipes, a bugle and fiddles
tipping their bellies (round as the thick-
sided glasses whose wash they impound)
their hips and their bellies off balance
to turn them. Kicking and rolling about
the Fair Grounds, swinging their butts, those
shanks must be sound to bear up under such
rollicking measures, prance as they dance
in Breughel's great picture, The Kermess.

The Quality of Heaven

        Without other cost than breath
        and the poor soul,
        carried in the cage of the ribs,
        chirping shrilly

        I walked in the garden. The
        garden smelled of roses.
        The lilies' green throats opened
        to yellow trumpets

        that craved no sound and the rain
        was fresh in my face,
        the air a sweet breath.

                          Yesterday
      the heat was oppressive

      dust clogged the leaves' green
      and bees from
      the near hive, parched, drank,
      overeager, at

      the birdbath and were drowned there.
      Others replaced them
      from which the birds were
      frightened.
                —the fleece-light air!

Ol' Bunk's Band

These are men! the gaunt, unfore-
    sold, the vocal,
blatant, Stand up, stand up! the
    slap of a bass-string.
Pick, ping! The horn, the
    hollow horn
long drawn out, a hound deep
    tone—
Choking, choking! while the
    treble reed
races—alone, ripples, screams
    slow to fast—
to second to first! These are men!

Drum, drum, drum, drum, drum
    drum, drum! the
ancient cry, escaping crapulence
    eats through
transcendent—torn, tears, term
    town, tense,
turns and back off whole, leaps
    up, stomps down,
rips through! These are men
    beneath
whose force the melody limps—
    to
proclaim, proclaims—Run and
    lie down,
in slow measures, to rest and
    not never
need no more! These are men!
    Men!

The Visit

>I have committed many errors
but I warn—the interplay
is not the tossed body. Though
the mind is subtler than the sea,
advancing at three speeds,
the fast, the medium and the slow,
recapitulating at every ninth
wave what was not at first directly
stated, that is still only
on the one level.

>>There are the fish
and at the bottom, the ground,
no matter whether at five feet
or five miles, the ground, revealing,
when bared by the tides, living
barnacles, hungry on the rocks
as the mind is, that hiss as often
loudly when the sun bites them.

>And I acknowledge, the mind is
still (though rarely) more than
its play. I can see also
the dagger in the left hand when
the right strikes. It does
not alter the case.

>Let us resume. The
naive may be like a sunny day
deceptive
and is not to be despised
because it is so amusing to see
the zigzag and slender gulls

dip
into the featureless surface.
It is fish they are after,
fish—and get them.

                Still I
acknowledge the sea is there **and**
I admire its profundity only
what does that amount to?
Love also may be deep, deep
as thought, deeper than thought
and as sequential—

                thought
full of detail, let us say, as
the courts are full of law
and the sea, weeds and
as murmurous: that does **not**
alter the case either. Yet you
are right in the end: law
often decides cases. Well?
I prefer to go back to my **cases**
at the hospital.

Say I am less an artist
than a spadeworker but one
who has no aversion to taking
his spade to the head
of any who would derrogate
his performance in the craft.

You were kind to be at such
pains with me and—thanks
for the view.

Aigeltinger

In the bare trees old husks make new designs
Love moves the crows before the dawn
The cherry-sun ushers in the new phase

The radiant mind
addressed by tufts of flocking pear blossoms
proposes new profundities to the soul

Deftness stirs in the cells
of Aigeltinger's brain which flares
like ribbons round an electric fan

This is impressive, he will soon proclaim
God!

And round and round, the winds
and underfoot, the grass
the rose-cane leaves and blackberries
and Jim will read the encyclopedia to his
new bride—gradually

Aigeltinger you have stuck in my conk
illuminating, for nearly half a century I
could never beat you at your specialty

Nothing has ever beaten a mathematician
but yeast

The cloudless sky takes the sun in its periphery
and slides its disc across the blue

They say I'm not profound

But where is profundity, Aigeltinger
mathematical genius
dragged drunk from some cheap bar to serve
their petty purposes?

Aigeltinger, you were profound

The Injury

       From this hospital bed
       I can hear an engine
       breathing—somewhere
           in the night:

       —Soft coal, soft coal,
           soft coal!

       And I know it is men
           breathing
       shoveling, resting—

       —Go about it
       the slow way, if you can
       find any way—
               Christ!
       who's a bastard?
               —quit
       and quit shoveling.

       A man breathing
           and it quiets and
       the puff of steady

work begins
            slowly: Chug.
Chug. Chug. Chug. . . .
            fading off.
Enough coal at least
        for this small job

    Soft! Soft!
—enough for one small
engine, enough for that.

A man shoveling
working and not lying here
        in this
hospital bed—powerless
—with the white-throat
        calling in the
poplars before dawn, his
faint flute-call,
triple tongued, piercing
the shingled curtain
of the new leaves;
        drowned out by
        car wheels
singing now on the rails,
taking the curve,
    slowly,
        a long wail,
high pitched:
        rounding
            the curve—
—the slow way because
(if you can find any way) that is
the only way left now
                for you.

Franklin Square

Instead of
the flower of the hawthorn
the spine:

The tree is in bloom
the flowers
and the leaves together

sheltering
the noisy sparrows
that give

by their intimate
indifference,
the squirrels and pigeons

on the sharp-
edged lawns—the figure
of a park:

A city, a decadence
of bounty—
a tall negress approaching

the bench
pursing her old mouth
for what coin?

Choral: the Pink Church

      Pink as a dawn in Galilee
      whose stabbing fingers routed
      Aeschylus and murder blinked . . .

      —and tho' I remember little
          as names go,
      the thrust of that first light
          was to me
          as through a heart
          of jade—
      as chinese as you please
      but not by that—remote

      Now,
          the Pink Church
              trembles
      to the light (of dawn) again,
          rigors of more
          than sh'd wisely
          be said at one stroke,
      singing!
          Covertly.
                  Subdued.

        Sing!
      transparent to the light
          through which the light
      shines, through the stone,
          until
      the stone-light glows,
          pink jade
      —that is the light and is
          a stone

and is a church—if the image
    hold . . .

as at a breath a face glows
    and fades!
Come all ye aberrant,
    drunks, prostitutes,
    Surrealists—
    Gide and—
Proust's memory (in a cork
    diving suit
looking under the sea
        of silence)
to bear witness:

Man is not sinful . . . unless
    he sin!
—Poe, Whitman, Baudelaire
    the saints
        of this calendar.

Oh ladies whose beds
    your
husbands defile! man, man
    is the bringer
    of pure delights
    to you!

Who else?

    And there stand
    the-banded-together
    in the name of
    the Philosophy Dep'ts

wondering at the nature

                of the stuff
                poured into
                the urinals
                        of custom . . .

O Dewey! (John)
    O James! (William)
        O Whitehead!
                teach well!
—above and beyond
    your teaching stands
the Pink Church:
            the nipples of
a woman who never
    bore a
        child . . .

Oh what new vows shall
we swear to make all swearing
futile:
        the fool
        the mentally deranged
        the suicide?

—suckled of its pink delight

And beyond them all whine
the slaughtered, the famished
and the lonely—
    the holy church of
their minds singing madly
    in tune, its stones
sibilant and roaring—

                Soft voiced . . .

To which, double bass:

A torch to a heap
    of new branches
    under the tied feet of
    Michael Servitus:

        Be ye therefore perfect
        even as your
        Father in Heaven
        is perfect

And all you liveried bastards,
    all (tho' pardon me
    all you who come
    rightly under that holy
    term)

        Harken!

—perfect as the pink and
    rounded breasts of a virgin!
Scream it in
        their stupid ears—
plugged by wads of
newspulp—

        Joy! Joy!
        —out of Elysium!

—chanted loud as a chorus from
    the Agonistes—

Milton, the unrhymer,
        singing among
            the rest . . .

like a Communist.

Lear

When the world takes over for us
and the storm in the trees
replaces our brittle consciences
(like ships, female to all seas)
when the few last yellow leaves
stand out like flags on tossed ships
at anchor—our minds are rested

Yesterday we sweated and dreamed
or sweated in our dreams walking
at a loss through the bulk of figures
that appeared solid, men or women,
but as we approached down the paved
corridor melted—Was it I?—like
smoke from bonfires blowing away

Today the storm, inescapable, has
taken the scene and we return
our hearts to it, however made, made
wives by it and though we secure
ourselves for a dry skin from the drench
of its passionate approaches we
yield and are made quiet by its fury

Pitiful Lear, not even you could
out-shout the storm—to make a fool
cry! Wife to its power might you not
better have yielded earlier? as on ships
facing the seas were carried once
the figures of women at repose to
signify the strength of the waves' lash.

The Horse Show

Constantly near you, I never in my entire
sixty-four years knew you so well as yesterday
or half so well. We talked. You were never
so lucid, so disengaged from all exigencies
of place and time. We talked of ourselves,
intimately, a thing never heard of between us.
How long have we waited? almost a hundred years.

You said, Unless there is some spark, some
spirit we keep within ourselves, life, a
continuing life's impossible—and it is all
we have. There is no other life, only the one.
The world of the spirits that comes afterward
is the same as our own, just like you sitting
there they come and talk to me, just the same.

They come to bother us. Why? I said. I don't
know. Perhaps to find out what we are doing.
Jealous, do you think? I don't know. I
don't know why they should want to come back.
I was reading about some men who had been
buried under a mountain, I said to her, and
one of them came back after two months,

digging himself out. It was in Switzerland,
you remember? Of course I remember. The
villagers tho't it was a ghost coming down
to complain. They were frightened. They
do come, she said, what you call
my "visions." I talk to them just as I
am talking to you. I see them plainly.

Oh if I could only read! You don't know
what adjustments I have made. All
I can do is to try to live over again
what I knew when your brother and you
were children—but I can't always succeed.
Tell me about the horse show. I have
been waiting all week to hear about it.

Mother darling, I wasn't able to get away.
Oh that's too bad. It was just a show;
they make the horses walk up and down
to judge them by their form. Oh is that
all? I tho't it was something else. Oh
they jump and run too. I wish you had been
there, I was so interested to hear about it.

A Unison

The grass is very green, my friend,
and tousled, like the head of—
your grandson, yes? And the mountain,
the mountain we climbed
twenty years since for the last
time (I write this thinking
of you) is saw-horned as then
upon the sky's edge—an old barn
is peaked there also, fatefully,
against the sky. And there it is
and we can't shift it or change
it or parse it or alter it
in any way. *Listen! Do you not hear
them? the singing?* There it is and
we'd better acknowledge it and

write it down, not otherwise.
Not twist the words to mean
what we should have said but to mean
—what cannot be escaped: the
mountain riding the afternoon as
it does, the grass matted green,
green underfoot and the air—
rotten wood. *Hear! Hear them!
the Undying.* The hill slopes away,
then rises in the middleground,
you remember, with a grove of gnarled
maples centering the bare pasture,
sacred, surely—for what reason?
I cannot say? Idyllic!
a shrine cinctured there by
the trees, a certainty of music!
a unison and a dance, joined
at this death's festival: Something
of a shed snake's skin, the beginning
goldenrod. Or, best, a white stone,
you have seen it: *Mathilda Maria
Fox*—and near the ground's lip,
all but undecipherable, *Aet Suae
Anno 9*—still there, the grass
dripping of last night's rain—and
welcome! The thin air, the near,
clear brook water!—and could not,
and died, unable; to escape
what the air and the wet grass—
through which, tomorrow, bejeweled,
the great sun will rise—the
unchanging mountains, forced on them—
and they received, willingly!
Stones, stones of a difference
joining the others, at pace. *Hear!
Hear the unison of their voices....*

The Lion

1

Traffic, the lion, the sophisticate,
facing the primitive, alabaster,
the new fallen snow
stains its chastity the new shade

Use defames! the attack disturbs our sleep

This is the color of the road, the color
of the lion, sand color

—to follow the lion, of use or usage,
even to church! the bells achime
above the fallen snow!

—all follow the same road, space.

2

Winter, the churned snow, the lion
flings the woman, taking her
by the throat upon his gullied
shoulders—shaking the weight fast
and unmolested plunges with her
among the trees—where the whiteness
sparkles—to devour her there:
transit to uses: where the traffic
mounts, a chastity packed with lewdness,
a rule, dormant, against the loosely
fallen snow—the thick muscles

working under the skin, the head
like a tree-stump, gnawing: chastity
to employment, lying down bloodied
to bed together for the last time.

The Three Graces

We have the picture of you in mind,
when you were young, posturing
(for a photographer) in scarves
(if you could have done it) but now,
for none of you is immortal, ninety-
three, the three, ninety and three,
Mary, Ellen and Emily, what
beauty is it clings still about you?
Undying? Magical? For there is still
no answer, why we live or why
you will not live longer than I
or that there should be an answer why
any should live and whatever other
should die. Yet you live. You live
and all that can be said is that
you live, time cannot alter it—
and as I write this Mary has died.

The Descent

    The descent beckons
             as the ascent beckoned.
                      Memory is a kind
of accomplishment,
        a sort of renewal
                even
an initiation, since the spaces it opens are new places
        inhabited by hordes
                heretofore unrealized,
of new kinds—
        since their movements
                are toward new objectives
(even though formerly they were abandoned).

No defeat is made up entirely of defeat—since
the world it opens is always a place
        formerly
                unsuspected. A
world lost,
        a world unsuspected,
                beckons to new places
and no whiteness (lost) is so white as the memory
of whiteness

With evening, love wakens
        though its shadows
                which are alive by reason
of the sun shining—
        grow sleepy now and drop away
                from desire

Love without shadows stirs now
            beginning to awaken
                        as night
advances.

The descent
        made up of despairs
                and without accomplishment
realizes a new awakening:
                which is a reversal
of despair.
        For what we cannot accomplish, what
is denied to love,
        what we have lost in the anticipation—
                a descent follows,
endless and indestructible

To Daphne and Virginia

The smell of the heat is boxwood
        when rousing us
               a movement of the air
stirs our thoughts
        that had no life in them
               to a life, a life in which
two women agonize:
        to live and to breathe is no less.
                Two young women.
The box odor
        is the odor of that of which
                partaking separately,

> each to herself
> > I partake also
> > > . .   separately.

Be patient that I address you in a poem,
> there is no other
> > fit medium.

The mind
> lives there. It is uncertain,
> > can trick us and leave us

agonized. But for resources
> what can equal it?
> > There is nothing. We

should be lost
> without its wings to
> > fly off upon.

The mind is the cause of our distresses
> but of it we can build anew.
> > Oh something more than

it flies off to:
> a woman's world,
> > of crossed sticks, stopping

thought. A new world
> is only a new mind.
> > And the mind and the poem

are all apiece.
> Two young women
> > to be snared,

odor of box,
> to bind and hold them
> > for the mind's labors.

All women are fated similarly
> facing men
> > and there is always

another, such as I,
>   who loves them,
>   >   loves all women, but
finds himself, touching them,
>   like other men,
>   >   often confused.

I have two sons,
>   the husbands of these women,
>   >   who live also
in a world of love,
>   apart.
>   >   Shall this odor of box in
>   >   the heat
not also touch them
>   fronting a world of women
>   >   from which they are
debarred
>   by the very scents which draw them on
>   >   against easy access?
In our family we stammer unless,
>   half mad,
>   >   we come to speech at last

And I am not
>   a young man.
>   >   My love encumbers me.
It is a love
>   less than
>   >   a young man's love but,
like this box odor
>   more penetrant, infinitely
>   >   more penetrant,
in that sense not to be resisted.

            There is, in the hard
                        give and take
                                    of a man's life with
                            a woman
            a thing which is not the stress itself
                        but beyond
                                    and above
that,
            something that wants to rise
                        and shake itself
free. We are not chickadees
            on a bare limb
                        with a worm in the mouth.
The worm is in our brains
            and concerns them
                        and not food for our
offspring, wants to disrupt
            our thought
                        and throw it
to the newspapers
            or anywhere.
                        There is, in short,
a counter stress,
            born of the sexual shock,
                        which survives it
consonant with the moon,
            to keep its own mind.
                        There is, of course,
more.
            Women
                        are not alone
in that. At least
            while this healing odor is abroad
                        one can write a poem.

Staying here in the country
            on an old farm
                        we eat our breakfasts
on a balcony under an elm.
            The shrubs below us
                        are neglected. And
there, penned in,
            or he would eat the garden,
                        lives a pet goose who
tilts his head
            sidewise
                        and looks up at us,
a very quiet old fellow
            who writes no poems.
                        Fine mornings we sit there
while birds
            come and go.
                        A pair of robins
is building a nest
            for the second time
                        this season. Men
against their reason
            speak of love, sometimes,
                        when they are old. It is
all they can do
            or watch a heavy goose
                        who waddles, slopping
                        noisily in the mud of
                        his pool.

The Sparrow

(*To My Father*)

This sparrow
>who comes to sit at my window
>>is a poetic truth
more than a natural one.
>His voice,
>>his movements,
his habits—
>how he loves to
>>flutter his wings
in the dust—
>all attest it;
>>granted, he does it
to rid himself of lice
>but the relief he feels
>>makes him
cry out lustily—
>which is a trait
>>more related to music
than otherwise.
>>Wherever he finds himself
>>>in early spring,
on back streets
>or beside palaces,
>>he carries on
unaffectedly
>his amours.
>>It begins in the egg,
his sex genders it:
>What is more pretentiously
>>useless
or about which
>we more pride ourselves?

                        It leads as often as not
to our undoing.
            The cockerel, the crow
                        with their challenging voices
cannot surpass
            the insistence
                        of his cheep!
Once
            at El Paso
                        toward evening,
I saw—and heard!—
            ten thousand sparrows
                        who had come in from
the desert
            to roost. They filled the trees
                        of a small park. Men fled
(with ears ringing!)
            from their droppings,
                        leaving the premises
to the alligators
            who inhabit
                        the fountain. His image
is familiar
            as that of the aristocratic
                        unicorn, a pity
there are not more oats eaten
            nowadays
                        to make living easier
for him.
            At that,
                        his small size,
keen eyes,
            serviceable beak
                        and general truculence
assure his survival—
            to say nothing
                        of his innumerable

brood.
           Even the Japanese
                   know him
and have painted him
           sympathetically,
                   with profound insight
into his minor
           characteristics.
                   Nothing even remotely
subtle
           about his lovemaking.
                   He crouches
before the female,
           drags his wings,
                   waltzing,
throws back his head
           and simply—
                   yells! The din
is terrific.
           The way he swipes his bill
                   across a plank
to clean it,
       is decisive.
                   So with everything
he does. His coppery
           eyebrows
                   give him the air
of being always
           a winner—and yet
                   I saw once,
the female of his species
           clinging determinedly
                   to the edge of
a water pipe,
           catch him
                   by his crown-feathers

to hold him
        silent,
                subdued,
hanging above the city streets
        until
                she was through with him.
What was the use
        of that?
                She hung there
herself,
        puzzled at her success.
                I laughed heartily.
Practical to the end,
        it is the poem
                of his existence
that triumphed
        finally;
                a wisp of feathers
flattened to the pavement,
        wings spread symmetrically
                as if in flight,
the head gone,
        the black escutcheon of the breast
                undecipherable,
an effigy of a sparrow,
        a dried wafer only,
                left to say
and it says it
        without offense,
                beautifully;
This was I,
        a sparrow.
                I did my best;
farewell.

Asphodel, That Greeny Flower

BOOK I

Of asphodel, that greeny flower,
          like a buttercup
                    upon its branching stem—
save that it's green and wooden—
          I come, my sweet,
                    to sing to you.
We lived long together
          a life filled,
                    if you will,
with flowers. So that
          I was cheered
                    when I came first to know
that there were flowers also
          in hell.
                    Today
I'm filled with the fading memory of those flowers
          that we both loved,
                    even to this poor
colorless thing—
          I saw it
                    when I was a child—
little prized among the living
          but the dead see,
                    asking among themselves:
What do I remember
          that was shaped
                    as this thing is shaped?
while our eyes fill
          with tears.
                    Of love, abiding love
it will be telling

                    though too weak a wash of crimson
                              colors it
to make it wholly credible.
                    There is something
                              something urgent
I have to say to you
          and you alone
                    but it must wait
while I drink in
          the joy of your approach,
                    perhaps for the last time.
And so
          with fear in my heart
                    I drag it out
and keep on talking
          for I dare not stop.
                    Listen while I talk on
against time.
          It will not be
                    for long.
I have forgot
          and yet I see clearly enough
                    something
central to the sky
          which ranges round it.
                    An odor
springs from it!
          A sweetest odor!
                    Honeysuckle! And now
there comes the buzzing of a bee!
          and a whole flood
                    of sister memories!
Only give me time,
          time to recall them
                    before I shall speak out.
Give me time,
          time.

143

When I was a boy
        I kept a book
                to which, from time
to time,
        I added pressed flowers
                until, after a time,
I had a good collection.
        The asphodel,
                forebodingly,
among them.
        I bring you,
                reawakened,
a memory of those flowers.
        They were sweet
                when I pressed them
and retained
        something of their sweetness
                a long time.
It is a curious odor,
        a moral odor,
                that brings me
near to you.
        The color
                was the first to go.
There had come to me
        a challenge,
                your dear self,
mortal as I was,
        the lily's throat
                to the hummingbird!
Endless wealth,
        I thought,
                held out its arms to me.
A thousand topics
        in an apple blossom.
                The generous earth itself

gave us lief.
        The whole world
                became my garden!
But the sea
        which no one tends
               is also a garden
when the sun strikes it
        and the waves
               are wakened.
I have seen it
        and so have you
               when it puts all flowers
to shame.
        Too, there are the starfish
                stiffened by the sun
and other sea wrack
        and weeds. We knew that
                along with the rest of it
for we were born by the sea,
        knew its rose hedges
                to the very water's brink.
There the pink mallow grows
        and in their season
               strawberries
and there, later,
        we went to gather
               the wild plum.
I cannot say
        that I have gone to hell
                for your love
but often
        found myself there
               in your pursuit.
I do not like it
        and wanted to be
               in heaven. Hear me out.

Do not turn away.

I have learned much in my life
        from books
                and out of them
about love.
        Death
                is not the end of it.
There is a hierarchy
        which can be attained,
                I think,
in its service.
        Its guerdon
                is a fairy flower;
a cat of twenty lives.
        If no one came to try it
                the world
would be the loser.
        It has been
                for you and me
as one who watches a storm
        come in over the water.
                We have stood
from year to year
        before the spectacle of our lives
                with joined hands.
The storm unfolds.
        Lightning
                plays about the edges of the clouds.
The sky to the north
        is placid,
                blue in the afterglow
as the storm piles up.
        It is a flower
                that will soon reach
the apex of its bloom.
        We danced,

                        in our minds,
and read a book together.
            You remember?
                        It was a serious book.
And so books
            entered our lives.
The sea! The sea!
            Always
                        when I think of the sea
there comes to mind
            the *Iliad*
                        and Helen's public fault
that bred it.
            Were it not for that
                        there would have been
no poem but the world
            if we had remembered,
                        those crimson petals
spilled among the stones,
            would have called it simply
                        murder.
The sexual orchid that bloomed then
            sending so many
                        disinterested
men to their graves
            has left its memory
                        to a race of fools
or heroes
            if silence is a virtue.
                        The sea alone
with its multiplicity
            holds any hope.
                        The storm
has proven abortive
            but we remain
                        after the thoughts it roused

to
              re-cement our lives.
                        It is the mind
the mind
              that must be cured
                        short of death's
intervention,
         and the will becomes again
                   a garden. The poem
is complex and the place made
              in our lives
                        for the poem.
Silence can be complex too,
         but you do not get far
                        with silence.
Begin again.
              It is like Homer's
                        catalogue of ships:
it fills up the time.
         I speak in figures,
                   well enough, the dresses
you wear are figures also,
         we could not meet
                   otherwise. When I speak
of flowers
         it is to recall
                   that at one time
we were young.
         All women are not Helen,
                   I know that,
but have Helen in their hearts.
         My sweet,
                   you have it also, therefore
I love you
         and could not love you otherwise.
                   Imagine you saw

a field made up of women
             all silver-white.
                          What should you do
but love them?
             The storm bursts
                          or fades! it is not
the end of the world.
             Love is something else,
                          or so I thought it,
a garden which expands,
             though I knew you as a woman
                          and never thought otherwise,
until the whole sea
             has been taken up
                          and all its gardens.
It was the love of love,
             the love that swallows up all else,
                          a grateful love,
a love of nature, of people,
             animals,
                          a love engendering
gentleness and goodness
             that moved me
                          and *that* I saw in you.
I should have known
             though I did not,
                          that the lily-of-the-valley
is a flower makes many ill
             who whiff it.
                          We had our children,
rivals in the general onslaught.
             I put them aside
                          though I cared for them
as well as any man
             could care for his children
                          according to my lights.

  You understand
     I had to meet you
        after the event
and have still to meet you.
     Love
        to which you too shall bow
along with me—
    a flower
       a weakest flower
shall be our trust
     and not because
        we are too feeble
to do otherwise
    but because
        at the height of my power
I risked what I had to do,
    therefore to prove
       that we love each other
while my very bones sweated
    that I could not cry to you
       in the act.
Of asphodel, that greeny flower,
    I come, my sweet,
        to sing to you!
My heart rouses
    thinking to bring you news
       of something
that concerns you
    and concerns many men. Look at
       what passes for the new.
You will not find it there but in
    despised poems.
       It is difficult
to get the news from poems
     yet men die miserably every day
        for lack

of what is found there.
           Hear me out
                      for I too am concerned
and every man
           who wants to die at peace in his bed
                      besides.

CODA

Inseparable from the fire
           its light
                      takes precedence over it.
Then follows
           what we have dreaded—
                      but it can never
overcome what has gone before.
           In the huge gap
                      between the flash
and the thunderstroke
           spring has come in
                      or a deep snow fallen.
Call it old age.
           In that stretch
                      we have lived to see
a colt kick up his heels.
           Do not hasten
                      laugh and play
in an eternity
           the heat will not overtake the light.
                      That's sure.
That gelds the bomb,
           permitting
                      that the mind contain it.

This is that interval,
        that sweetest interval,
                when love will blossom,
come early, come late
        and give itself to the lover.
Only the imagination is real!
        I have declared it
               time without end.
If a man die
        it is because death
               has first
possessed his imagination.
        But if he refuse death—
               no greater evil
can befall him
        unless it be the death of love
               meet him
in full career.
        Then indeed
               for him
the light has gone out.
But love and the imagination
        are of a piece,
               swift as the light
to avoid destruction.
        So we come to watch time's flight
               as we might watch
summer lightning
        or fireflies, secure,
               by grace of the imagination,
safe in its care.
        For if
               the light itself
has escaped,
        the whole edifice opposed to it
               goes down.

                Light, the imagination
                            and love,
                                        in our age,
                by natural law,
                            which we worship,
                                        maintain
                all of a piece
                            their dominance.
                So let us love
                            confident as is the light
                                        in its struggle with darkness
                that there is as much to say
                            and more
                                        for the one side
                and that not the darker
                            which John Donne
                                        for instance
                among many men
                            presents to us.
                                        In the controversy
                touching the younger
                            and the older Tolstoi,
                                        Villon, St. Anthony, Kung,
                Rimbaud, Buddha
                            and Abraham Lincoln
                                        the palm goes
                always to the light;
                            Who most shall advance the light—
                                        call it what you may!
                The light
                            for all time shall outspeed
                                        the thunder crack.
                Medieval pageantry
                            is human and we enjoy
                                        the rumor of it

          as in our world we enjoy
                    the reading of Chaucer,
                              likewise
a priest's raiment
          (or that of a savage chieftain).
                    It is all
a celebration of the light.
          All the pomp and ceremony
                    of weddings,
"Sweet Thames, run softly
          till I end
                    my song,"—
are of an equal sort.
For our wedding, too,
          the light was wakened
                    and shone. The light!
the light stood before us
          waiting!
                    I thought the world
stood still.
          At the altar
                    so intent was I
before my vows,
          so moved by your presence
                    a girl so pale
and ready to faint
          that I pitied
                    and wanted to protect you.
As I think of it now,
          after a lifetime,
                    it is as if
a sweet-scented flower
          were poised
                    and for me did open.

Asphodel
        has no odor
                save to the imagination
but it too
        celebrates the light.
                It is late
but an odor
        as from our wedding
                has revived for me
and begun again to penetrate
        into all crevices
                of my world.

The Lady Speaks

A storm raged among the live oaks
        while my husband and I
                sat in the semi-dark
listening!
        We watched from the windows,
                the lights off,
saw the moss
        whipped upright
                by the wind's force.
Two candles we had lit
        side by side
                before us
so solidly had our house been built
        kept their tall flames
                unmoved.
May it be so
        when a storm sends the moss
                whipping

>   back and forth
>   upright
>   above my head
>   like flames in the final
>   fury.

A Negro Woman

           carrying a bunch of marigolds
                   wrapped
                           in an old newspaper:
           She carries them upright,
                   bareheaded,
                           the bulk
           of her thighs
                   causing her to waddle
                           as she walks
           looking into
                   the store window which she passes
                           on her way.
           What is she
                   but an ambassador
                           from another world
           a world of pretty marigolds
                   of two shades
                           which she announces
           not knowing what she does
                   other
                           than walk the streets
           holding the flowers upright
                   as a torch
                           so early in the morning.

Shadows

I

Shadows cast by the street light
             under the stars,
                         the head is tilted back,
the long shadow of the legs
             presumes a world
                         taken for granted
on which the cricket trills.
             The hollows of the eyes
                         are unpeopled.
Right and left
             climb the ladders of night
                         as dawn races
to put out the stars.
             That
                         is the poetic figure
but we know
             better: what is not now
                         will never
be. Sleep secure,
             the little dog in the snapshot
                         keeps his shrewd eyes
pared. Memory
             is liver than sight.
                         A man
looking out,
             seeing the shadows—
                         it is himself
that can be painlessly amputated
             by a mere shifting
                         of the stars.
A comfort so easily not to be

                and to be at once one
                            with every man.
The night blossoms
            with a thousand shadows
                        so long
as there are stars,
            street lights
                        or a moon and
who shall say
            by their shadows
which is different
            from the other
                        fat or lean.

                    II

Ripped from the concept of our lives
            and from all concept
                        somehow, and plainly,
the sun will come up
            each morning
                        and sink again.
So that we experience
            violently
                        every day
two worlds
            one of which we share with the
            rose in bloom
                        and one,
by far the greater,
            with the past,
                        the world of memory,
the silly world of history,
            the world
                        of the imagination.

    Which leaves only the beasts and trees,
            crystals
                        with their refractive
                        surfaces
and rotting things
        to stir our wonder.
                  Save for the little
central hole
        of the eye itself
                into which
we dare not stare too hard
        or we are lost.
                The instant
trivial as it is
        is all we have
                unless—unless
things the imagination feeds upon,
        the scent of the rose,
                startle us anew.

Pictures from Brueghel

      I   SELF-PORTRAIT

In a red winter hat blue
eyes smiling
just the head and shoulders

crowded on the canvas
arms folded one
big ear the right showing

the face slightly tilted
a heavy wool coat
with broad buttons

gathered at the neck reveals
a bulbous nose
but the eyes red-rimmed

from over-use he must have
driven them hard
but the delicate wrists

show him to have been a
man unused to
manual labor unshaved his

blond beard half trimmed
no time for any-
thing but his painting

III   THE HUNTERS IN THE SNOW

The over-all picture is winter
icy mountains
in the background the return

from the hunt it is toward evening
from the left
sturdy hunters lead in

their pack the inn-sign
hanging from a
broken hinge is a stag a crucifix

between his antlers the cold
inn yard is
deserted but for a huge bonfire

that flares wind-driven tended by
women who cluster
about it to the right beyond

the hill is a pattern of skaters
Brueghel the painter
concerned with it all has chosen

a winter-struck bush for his
foreground to
complete the picture .   .

VIII THE WEDDING DANCE IN THE OPEN AIR

Disciplined by the artist
to go round
& round

in holiday gear
a riotously gay rabble of
peasants and their

ample-bottomed doxies
fills
the market square

featured by the women in
their starched
white headgear

they prance or go openly
toward the wood's
edges

round and around in
rough shoes and
farm breeches

mouths agape
Oya!
kicking up their heels

IX THE PARABLE OF THE BLIND

This horrible but superb painting
the parable of the blind
without a red

in the composition shows a group
of beggars leading
each other diagonally downward

across the canvas
from one side
to stumble finally into a bog

where the picture
and the composition ends back
of which no seeing man

is represented the unshaven
features of the des-
titute with their few

pitiful possessions a basin
to wash in a peasant
cottage is seen and a church spire

the faces are raised
as toward the light
there is no detail extraneous

to the composition one
follows the others stick in
hand triumphant to disaster

X   CHILDREN'S GAMES

I

This is a schoolyard
crowded
with children

of all ages near a village
on a small stream
meandering by

where some boys
are swimming
bare-ass

or climbing a tree in leaf
everything
is motion

elder women are looking
after the small
fry

a play wedding a
christening
nearby one leans

hollering
into
an empty hogshead

Heel & Toe to the End

Gagarin says, in ecstasy,
he could have
gone on forever

he floated
ate and sang
and when he emerged from that

one hundred eight minutes off
the surface of
the earth he was smiling

Then he returned
to take his place
among the rest of us

from all that division and
subtraction a measure
toe and heel

heel and toe he felt
as if he had
been dancing

An Exercise

Sick as I am
confused in the head
I mean I have

endured this April
so far
visiting friends

returning home
late at night
I saw

a huge Negro
a dirty collar
about his

enormous neck
appeared to be
choking

him
I did not know
whether or not

he saw me though
he was sitting
directly

before me how
shall we
escape this modern

age
and learn
to breathe again

The Dance

When the snow falls the flakes
spin upon the long axis
that concerns them most intimately
two and two to make a dance

the mind dances with itself,
taking you by the hand,
your lover follows
there are always two,

yourself and the other,
the point of your shoe setting the pace,
if you break away and run
the dance is over

Breathlessly you will take
another partner
better or worse who will keep
at your side, at your stops

whirls and glides until he too
leaves off
on his way down as if
there were another direction

gayer, more carefree
spinning face to face but always down
with each other secure
only in each other's arms

But only the dance is sure!
make it your own.
Who can tell
what is to come of it?

in the woods of your
own nature whatever
twig interposes, and bare twigs
have an actuality of their own

this flurry of the storm
that holds us,
plays with us and discards us
dancing, dancing as may be credible.

The Snow Begins

A rain of bombs, well placed,
is no less lovely
but this comes gently over all

all crevices are covered
the stalks of
fallen flowers vanish before

this benefice all the garden's
wounds are healed
white, white, white as death

fallen which dignifies it as
no violence ever can
gently and silently in the night.

The Rewaking

Sooner or later
we must come to the end
of striving

to re-establish
the image the image of
the rose

but not yet
you say extending the
time indefinitely

by
your love until a whole
spring

rekindle
the violet to the very
lady's-slipper

and so by
your love the very sun
itself is revived

Paul

I

when you shall arrive
as deep
as you will need go

to catch the blackfish
the hook
has been featly baited

by the art you have
and
you do catch them

II

with what thoroughness
you know
seize that glistening

body translated
to
that language you

will understand gut
clean
roast garnish and

III

serve to yourself who
better
eat and enjoy

however you
divide
and share

that blackfish heft
and shine
is your own

Song

> beauty is a shell
> from the sea
> where she rules triumphant
> till love has had its way with her
>
> scallops and
> lion's paws
> sculptured to the
> tune of retreating waves
>
> undying accents
> repeated till
> the ear and the eye lie
> down together in the same bed

The High Bridge above the Tagus River at Toledo

A young man, alone, on the high bridge over the Tagus which
    was too narrow to allow the sheep driven by the lean,
    enormous dogs whose hind legs worked slowly on cogs
to pass easily . . .
    (he didn't speak the language)

Pressed against the parapet either side by the crowding sheep,
    the relentless pressure of the dogs communicated
       itself to him also
above the waters in the gorge below.

They were hounds to him rather than sheep dogs because of
 their size and savage appearance, dog tired from the day's
 work.
The stiff jerking movement of the hind legs, the hanging
 heads at the shepherd's heels, slowly followed the excited
 and crowding sheep.

The whole flock, the shepherd and the dogs, were covered
 with dust as if they had been all day long on the road. The
 pace of the sheep, slow in the mass,
governed the man and the dogs. They were approaching the
 city at nightfall, the long journey completed.

In old age they walk in the old man's dreams and still walk
 in his dreams, peacefully continuing in his verse
 forever.

The Gift

        As the wise men of old brought gifts
            guided by a star
                to the humble birthplace

of the god of love,
      the devils
           as an old print shows
retreated in confusion.

        What could a baby know
           of gold ornaments
or frankincense and myrrh,
        of priestly robes
             and devout genuflections?

But the imagination
> knows all stories
>> before they are told
and knows the truth of this one
> past all defection

The rich gifts
> so unsuitable for a child
>> though devoutly proffered,
stood for all that love can bring.

> The men were old
>> how could they know
of a mother's needs
> or a child's
> appetite?

But as they kneeled
> the child was fed.
>> They saw it
and
> gave praise!

> A miracle
had taken place,
> hard gold to love,
a mother's milk!
> before
>> their wondering eyes.

The ass brayed
> the cattle lowed.
>> It was their nature.

All men by their nature give praise.
    It is all
        they can do.

The very devils
    by their flight give praise.
        What is death,
beside this?

    Nothing. The wise men
        came with gifts
and bowed down
    to worship
        this perfection.

The Woodthrush

fortunate man it is not too late
the woodthrush
flies into my garden

before the snow
he looks at me silent without
moving

his dappled breast reflecting
tragic winter
thoughts my love my own

To Be Recited to Flossie on Her Birthday

Let him who may
among the continuing lines
seek out

that tortured constancy
affirms
where I persist

let me say
across cross purposes
that the flower bloomed

struggling to assert itself
simply under
the conflicting lights

you will believe me
a rose
to the end of time